CREATIVE WRITING
IN THE
ELEMENTARY SCHOOL

2

MINED!"

"I want bussness
bussness bussness
bus------^" but sir
thats what I got, I-----"
"quite inturruping
I want ---- you said
you had bussness"? "yes sir big
bussness.
"Give me the lowdown"
'well you see boss in Africa
there has been descovered
a kind of porkipine it is
ficured that pichters of
this bird could be sold
to musums at milloons of
dollars each!" The bosses
eyes whent blank

WOW!

CREATIVE WRITING
IN THE
ELEMENTARY SCHOOL

Psychology and Technique

Don Pease

An Exposition–University Book

EXPOSITION PRESS   NEW YORK

EXPOSITION PRESS INC., 386 Park Ave. South, New York, N.Y.

FIRST EDITION

EP 42009

To

children and teachers everywhere
who can grow through written experience;
and especially to
those students
who contributed the ideas and stories
used here

To

children and teachers everywhere

who can grow through written expression

and especially

those students

who contributed the ideas and stories

used here

CONTENTS

CREATIVE WRITING
IN THE
ELEMENTARY SCHOOL

Oh, teacher, use your tricks of the trade, your knowledge of how I grow, your untiring and ever-present ways of encouraging—use them all and *help me become.*

CHAPTER I

INTRODUCTION

Communication Forms in the Elementary Classroom

THAT the process of communication is many-faceted has been illustrated by James Brown when he likened communication to "four lanes of traffic": two lanes coming in—reading, listening—and two lanes carrying out—writing, speaking. The traffic on those lanes consists of ideas, feelings, facts, and other perceptual forms.*

Perhaps the major function of our schools is to aid in the development of these traffic lanes so that patterns of communication with other people and outside events can be sharpened as much as possible for all individuals in the school setting.

Much research has contributed to the development of the reading "lane of traffic." Basic skills, areas of difficulty, vocabularies, speed builders, and other aspects of curricular experience have greatly facilitated the development of reading programs in most elementary schools.

Activities dealing with the other three lanes—speech, listening, and writing—have been generally added to elementary programs in a helter-skelter manner, and for both continuity and quality have depended upon the specific teacher or group of

---

* James I. Brown, "Vocabulary—Key to Communication," *Education,* Vol. LXXX, No. 2 (October, 1959), pp. 80–84.

teachers guiding a particular program. Many teachers are constantly reading for new ideas to incorporate into their personal approach to building a well-rounded "communications program."

THE WRITING PROGRAM

Specifically, what is the "writing program" in the elementary school? A list of various types of writing that are experienced by elementary-school children includes—

Jingles	Newspapers
Rhymes	Themes
Jokes	Fictional stories
Anecdotes	Musicals
Riddles	Plays
Cartoons	Personal messages
Poems	Letters, business and
Legends	personal
Tables	Extra verses for songs
Directions	Project reports
Notices	Free writing, such as description

That the role of writing in any program is dependent upon the teacher is evident. Some teachers see more opportunities to work writing experiences into the ongoing program than others. Also, some teachers are more aware of techniques that will enable the child to improve in his writing ability, and these teachers are more likely than others to encourage student participation in various types of writing activities.

CHALLENGE TO EDUCATION

American education programs have generally set for themselves an enormous task—that of providing opportunity for the maximum growth and development of every individual of school age. From the very beginning, with the curriculum consisting of the three R's, writing has indeed been emphasized as an extremely important aspect of a child's education. The challenge is great to elementary-school teachers across the land—the challenge of helping each child to become more aware of his own potentialities for creative-writing expression, as well as helping children to become more aware of the basic needs for written expression in American society.

SKIMMING THE RESEARCH

Most of the writing and research concerning children's writing can be classified in three groups. First, attempts have been made to present the many kinds and styles of writing that children on all grade levels are demonstrably able to do. The collection, or anthology, or even the personal portfolio form the basis of this research; and it is usually presented without any interpretation or value judgment.

The second group of materials is concerned with the teaching of grammar. Many persons have tried to set the situation for teaching grammatical concepts. The whats, whens, and hows have been treated from a number of exploratory views.

A third large group of writings could be classified as "descriptive situations." Teachers have often written of single experiences. A description of the experience in rather informal style, with personal interpretation of the values or benefits derived, is a common pattern in writing.

Very little research has been carried out which has been concerned with the relationship of technique to teaching procedures and ability growth. No research has been found that provides teachers a resource list of the more effective techniques being used to motivate children toward writing stories.

To recognize that writing abilities are developed is important. In fact, recognition of the lack of research concerning certain questions pertinent to creative writing in elementary schools has given direction to the author's efforts. If writing *is* a process, what are the values and abilities pertinent to the process at the elementary-school level?

G. W. Wagner, at Iowa State Teachers College, summarized a writing workshop with a review of practices in schools today.

He quoted that a "gifted story teller is not so much 'gifted' as 'practiced.'"* What, then, are some of the practices that we as teachers might best use in guiding children to fuller development of their creative-writing abilities?

Other writings have suggested that the quality of a child's writings is related to the experiences that the child has had. Strickland writes, "The quality of what is expressed in writing depends upon the quality of thinking that undergirds it."† Neal R. Edmund notes that there seems to be a relationship between the prior experiences of fifth-grade children and the creative quality of their stories.‡

What, then, are characteristic experiences that would facilitate development of the child's writing abilities?

The questions asked here will serve as a basis for many considerations in later chapters. Before we proceed to these matters, some basic assumptions and definitions that are pertinent to this study will be attempted.

Concerning Frame of Reference

BASIC ASSUMPTIONS FOR CHILD DEVELOPMENT

The teacher takes a positive approach toward child growth and development. A child's efforts are seen as his best, whatever they may be, at least for that particular moment. A teacher working with children accepts each child for what he is, even though she will expect improvements in his future efforts. In accepting the present efforts of children, the teacher encourages children to develop attitudes favorable to trial and error, self-exploration,

---

* G. W. Wagner, "What Schools Are Doing in Creative Writing," *Education,* Vol. LXXIX (September, 1958), pp. 62–65.

† Ruth Strickland, "Evaluating Children's Composition," *Elementary English,* Vol. XXXVII, No. 5 (May, 1960), pp. 322–30.

‡ Neal R. Edmund, "The Relationship Between Prior Experience and the Creative Quality of Stories of Fifth Grade Children," *Elementary English,* Vol. XXV (April, 1958), pp. 248–49.

and exploration of new concepts and processes. The same teacher will often discourage such exploration by not respecting their efforts. It is also assumed that all children naturally want to improve their abilities in the areas we would have them work. Research indicates that nothing breeds success more than previous success does.

CREATIVITY

Persons having high potential for producing or contributing in socially accepted ways have been labeled "gifted," "talented," and "creative." These terms have in different instances been used to convey similar meanings. The term "creative" has been chosen for use here mainly because it still serves to indicate individuality and uniqueness.

However, even "creative" has been used to describe several characteristics or qualities of a person. In one instance the term serves to describe a person who is apparently endowed with something that ordinary people do not have. For example, some assume that a person may have been born with a natural creativeness in visual art, music, science, mathematics, or some other area of endeavor. From this point of view, some have it and some do not, depending upon heredity.

In a second instance, creativity is interpreted as being synonymous with high intelligence. Thus only the child with an extremely high I.Q. may have the capacity to become creative. Differences appear in the literature concerning the I.Q. above which a person is to be considered extremely capable. Terman places the dividing line at 140 I.Q.; other research indicates an I.Q. of 130 or 120 to be sufficient.

A third concept concerning the creative person more broadly defines "creativity" as a capacity for outstanding achievement in some area of human endeavor. Again, the areas of human endeavor would include art, music, science, and writing, among others. The emphasis in this concept is upon not only capacity, but also performance, for only through performance can such a person be recognized as being creative.

A fourth use of the term is the one that guides the purposes of this book. This general use of the word "creative" will refer to the effects of the child's efforts upon the child's entire personality. Creativity is seen as a process by which the child engages with his environment in an effort to become a better student, a more likable person, a more productive classmate, or, in this case, more proficient at self-expression through the medium of writing. Thus the following chapters will attempt to discuss the personal values, goals, patterns, strengths, and weaknesses that individuals encounter in an effort to become even more creative. Each child is considered by this interpretation to be unique, with individual modes of behavior that can be set in motion so that the child can become original and creative.

More specifically, creative writings are those which represent original efforts of a person, in this case a child. They may consist of original ideas—or of original organizations of ideas—but the important aspect of the writing is that it represents an extension of one or any of the child's own thought processes.

It is within this context that the following explorations of children's writings seem to have significant meaning—both for the children as they write, and for their guiding teachers.

ON RELATIVITY

Oh, relativity—
Fascinating cause
        of life's mysteries—
How dare you first love,
Then hate,
Then worry,
And then inspire!
Always involving,
        involving,
                involving,
And like a spider
        entwining a web of
                life itself—
Or like a waterfall,
        gushing with more energy
                and power
        than the fall can appreciate—
Or like the moon,
        so full
                and yet so far—
        so bright,
                but falsely so.

That we have known you
        in our small infinitesimal way
Is to have lived for a lifetime . . .
How ironic!
That nothing may seem too important—
        Yet everything seem so important!
That to seek but little
        Means to recognize so vast a fulfillment
                of time and space.

Oh, relativity,
  Let us comprehend your equations,
  Let us experience your most complicated
      intricacies—
  That we may truly be devoured by the concept
                        LIFE.

                    D.P.

CHAPTER II

WHY CHILDREN WRITE

MORE than ever, teachers today are trying to relate what the school program has to offer to the inner needs of the child. In efforts to make the experience as meaningful as possible, teachers are doing such things as—

Making allowances for individual differences in a variety of ways.

Attempting to adapt related materials to the child's level of comprehension.

Making use of field trips, audio-visual aids, etc., to add more "reality" to the problem being studied.

Teachers are also becoming more aware of the role played by values in the learning process. They have discovered that their own values help guide them in (1) the selection of experiences, (2) the selection of materials, (3) the expectancies they have for groups and for individuals. Almost every event that takes place in a classroom is value-guided.

What, then, are the child's values in relation to the topic we are discussing—that of story writing? How can we as teachers help the child relate his values to the task of improving his writing ability?

Figure 1 is a diagram to be used as a frame of reference throughout this chapter.

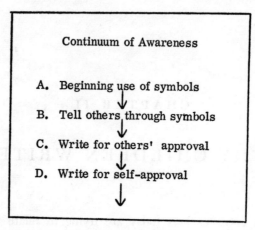

FIGURE 1. Values Guiding Children's Writings

Beginning Use of Symbols

A child's first use for symbols is an exciting one. He is only trying to make them. He is not expected to "communicate" with the first symbols the detailed, specific meanings that will be expected of him as he grows. He shows enthusiasm and interest as he makes symbols of all shapes and sizes, many of his own and some for the teacher. He can put his own personal meaning into his "system of symbols" because the teacher seems to be concerned not so much with the meaning portrayed as with the child's growth in motor control and his ability to draw a straight or a curved line. With freedom from outward criticism, the child's first experience of attaching personal meaning to symbology can be a very positive one.

To explore and make use of the child's value, then, the teacher need only do such things as—

Ask the child what meaning, if any, he has attached to his symbols.

Let him have the fun of explaining.

Help the child to see the relationship between his "symbol system" and any meaning that he has attached
to it. (This is what we all try to do later as we teach
reading and spelling.)

Several techniques (Chapter IV) will aid in guiding the child's
pursuit of this value.

As a child gains experience in relating meaning to his symbols, he will be eager to share his discoveries with others. It is
perhaps during this phase of "scribble writing" that a child is
most free with description and action. One teacher has described
the phase as follows.

The children liked to tell about the stories they had written
(through scribble writing). If the story they told was liked by
the class, they tended to add more and more things to tell. Sometimes the boys and girls asked questions about the stories, and
often the child looked in his "scribble story" for the answer.
Some children "read" the story directly from their writing. It
seemed a real thrill for them to be able to write about their experiences—and they seemed to know that "better ways of writing" would come later.

Perhaps we too would hope that "better ways of writing"
would come later, but we should consider meaningful experiences
that take place now and the role that such experiences will play
in the future writing patterns of the children.

The child continues to acquaint himself with the symbology
necessary for more effective communication. The excitement and
personal meaning that accompany this evolution of ideas enable
the child to experiment and write and share just for the sake of
experimenting and writing and sharing.

It appears, then, that throughout this period of "symbol exploration" the child is free from values other than his own for
the greatest part of his writing experience.

Telling Others Through Symbols

Ages eight, nine, and ten are increasingly exciting years for children. These ages are accompanied by a growing awareness of things outside themselves. Children become more aware, sometimes critically so, of the likes and dislikes of people around them. For many children the tendency is to carry moral teachings to extremes—trying to do things right according to group judgment, trying to make contributions that will please others, etc. In many ways this new "group consciousness" will affect a child's value selection—which in turn will affect the child's needs for writing.

How does this group consciousness seem to affect a child's writing patterns? One boy said that he liked to get "desired comments" from the children when he shared his stories. Another very sensitive child—one of the first children of his class to begin writing on his own—was now faced with writing things to please his classmates. Children of these ages generally want their writings to meet approval of members of the class as well as the teacher.

This value can be an incentive or a restriction for the child living by it. A well-adjusted child will take up the challenge of trying to write something that will be approved of. Some, however (such as the sensitive child just mentioned), will be careful and hesitant about writing because (as this same child felt) they can write only serious things, not the funny things that would be best accepted by others. Often the child sensitive to group approval and subject to it will try to avoid writing whenever he can.

A very effective technique in helping children to live with this value and still relate their efforts to writing is to have an occasional sharing period when any child who has written *may* put his efforts before his peers. Following each one's sharing, the teacher might ask, "How do you think Tommy has improved his stories today?" or, "Did any of you notice how Tommy did [this or that] to get the desired effect?" Teacher guidance should be positive in helping them discover their growth rather than to point out an eight-year-old's weaknesses.

With assurance that what he writes will be accepted for its positive aspects, the child will try to help others as he comments about the good things that occur in their writings.

Writing for the Approval of Others

Almost as soon as a child begins to write, he becomes conscious of the idea of "writing standards." Everyone around the child seems to have his own set of standards that indicate what good writing should be. The teacher has standards; the peers have standards; and the writer himself even has some ideas concerning the quality of a written story or poem. How this child reacts to the many sets of standards around him is in itself an interesting story, for some sets are in conflict with one another, some sets seem weaker than his own, and some sets are extremely difficult to satisfy.

TEACHER STANDARDS

As the child's own standards evolve, the teacher is apparently the earliest influence. In almost all areas of writing growth, the teacher's standards serve as a model for the child's written efforts during grades one, two, and three. For some children the same source will continue to give direction and meaning to their efforts in grades four and five. The child will seek teacher approval of his efforts as he tries to determine whether or not his efforts were good—or bad. A teacher's suggestion will appeal as a likely topic for most members of the class. The teacher's judgment of "the best writings" will be accepted as almost a universal law concerning the quality of what should be done.

That we teachers have helped the children to become dependent upon our ideals and standards will often serve at least two purposes. First, because at these ages (grades one to four) the children are naturally trying to analyze what our standards are—and then to live by them—we have the opportunity to challenge them with ideas representing growth and higher quality. With this first "golden" opportunity it appears that we often make one of two mistakes. By ignoring what we know about child psychology, and the many differences that characterize any group of twenty-five or thirty children, we continue to set the same standards for all students. This can be so unrealistic to some children that they will lose all interest in improving their own concept of what writing "really is." Also, as we help them to become dependent upon our standards, we often forget the eventual task to be done: that of helping each child to develop his own set of standards, then to subject them to continuous scrutiny in the light of new experience.

A second purpose in allowing children to be guided by the teacher's standards is more often observed. The teacher can set standards and ask the class to improve upon them. The children use the teacher's standards as a beginning point; then, as they become more critical of their own efforts, they will have opportunity to increase the meaningfulness of their standards.

PEER STANDARDS

The next stage in the development of a child's standards for story writing is to seek peer approval. For most children the model of authority seems to shift from the teacher to the peer group after the age of ten. Some children probably rely on the teacher's standards until they reach junior-high-school age, but the majority of them will be in a state of transferring their dependence to the peer group during the pre-adolescent years. (See Figure 2.)

How does this change in respect affect the child's standards for writing? Two very important reactions seem to occur. First, as children have opportunity to criticize the writings of other children objectively, they are exploring their own ideas about the standards that writing should meet. This implies that they then attempt to formulate a concept of what writing really is, from their own levels of insight—the insights which of necessity must guide their own written efforts. In this way the standards for children's writings will be realistic—and are much more likely to be practical enough to guide the individual child's written efforts.

A second reaction relates to aspects of discipline—motivation and reinforcement. Peers, by indicating approval of one's efforts, provide a most important incentive to the child whose actions are guided by peer approval. Peers can most effectively make suggestions and criticisms that will influence that child's future efforts. (It might appear that the child takes peer criticism even too seriously during these years; but teachers who are conscious of this behavior possibility must learn to work with this peer-approval value in relation to the positive growth experiences that can occur.)

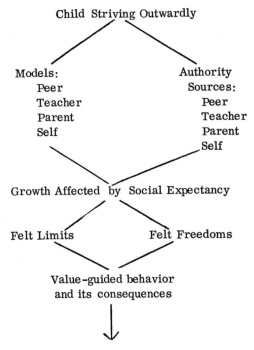

FIGURE 2. Growth in Relation to Models and Authority Sources

Writing for Self-expression

As children's concepts of and purposes for writing expand, the value of peer approval is replaced by self-approval and free self-expression. In this stage, they combine ideas at their own levels of insight as they continue to explore various writing patterns.

When a child criticizes his own writing, he is criticizing according to his own standards—from his best insight as to what writing really is. For the most meaningful learning to take place, it is almost necessary for a child to be critic of his own abilities, for only through analysis and criticism of these abilities do they have a chance for growth. As he listens to the stories of children with abilities similar to his own and as he critically notices the ideas and styles used, he will be better able to understand and improve his own style and technique. We as teachers want him to improve *his* concept of writing, perhaps even more than we want him to meet our standards for "what writing is."

This gradual evolution from teacher dependence to peer dependence to increasing self-dependence is a natural one, and will result from the child's awareness that his peers, like his teachers, are not always representative of the ultimate in "standard." Thus a growing child learns that he must depend upon his own judgment to an ever greater degree.

The author, as a teacher, was acquainted with several sixth-grade children who were intent on writing only for personally satisfying reasons. One pupil as a fifth-grader had written a science-fiction novelette of 167 pages in his own writing (including pictures). During his writing of this book (later published), he chose to read only occasionally to the rest of the class, and was rapidly accepting his writing as his own—and for his own purposes. This boy once said, "You get to use your imagination in expressing yourself. It's fun just to write down your ideas." The teacher once asked him if he thought he would like to write stories when he was older. He answered, "Oh, golly, yes. In my spare time I'll probably write a lot!"

Needless to say, only a few students will break away from the binds of peer approval in an elementary-school setting to be free to write just for self-expression. Indeed, few adults ever experience this high quality of personal achievement.

The values spoken of in this chapter seem to represent a continuum of growth—the guidelines by which children are likely to write in an elementary school. Perhaps the value pattern is representative of growth in any concept: (1) awareness and exploration, to which are added (2) purposes for action according to values. The values, as guides to purposes, evolve with the child's increasing awareness of his environment until he is free to select and accomplish, according to his own concepts, among the things that teachers would have him accomplish.

When asked what they liked about story writing, some children gave the following answers:

> I like to write my own stories and make them *come true on writing.* [Her stories were vividly concerned with true experiences.] Sometimes when I am writing I get so carried away I feel like they [her characters] are talking to me. I like to write about things that I would like to have happen to me and then add some things here and there. I love to write stories.
>
> I like stories that have a lot of imagination in them. Like in mine—I just start writing and as my thoughts get farther along I get new ideas.
>
> As for other people's stories, I enjoy the excitement and comedy in them. Some people's stories are just wonderful. Others—well, I won't comment. [Notice the ability to use his critical abilities in a positive, constructive way, thus allowing each of the other children to grow in his own way.]
>
> Well, I think it's fun to write stories. I like stories about animals the best.
>
> Well, I like it because it all almost comes to life in my point of view. I think if I listen hard to other people's stories, they come to life also.

You are free to express your ideas. You have fun playing with ideas. I like to hear other people's ideas, too.

I like it when some people try to express what they think through their stories.

I like silly stories because that is the kind I write about.

I can express my thoughts. I like to listen to other person's stories. I get my ideas from things that happened to me, things that might have happened to me, and from just plain thinking—and from just a funny idea.

I like story writing because it is a good way to say what you have imagined, what you know, what you feel towards some people and some places. I get my ideas from hearing things and seeing things.

These comments came from a single group of students who shared a wide range of writing abilities.

Casually now

An azure sky o'erhead, occasionally broken
   by soft trains of white, casts its spell.

The gentle breezes dance and play with the leaves and flowers—
   soothing and seething, their story to tell.

Such a day seems to open the barriers to living's fullness,
encouraging each creature capable of breath to quickly inhale
and take full measure of the beauty that lies within its personal world.

CHAPTER III

GROWTH:
THE SEQUENCE
OF STORY-WRITING ABILITIES

Characteristics of Growth

Is story writing an ability? Assuming that it is, is it possible to describe various stages of growth as indications that the ability is being developed?

In an elementary program in which the story writing abilities of children are given guidance through all of the grades, one might find the following indications of growth patterns and stages.

1. Scribble "writing"
2. Picture "writing"
3. Dictation to teacher
4. First word stories
5. Imitation and identification
6. Writing for self-expression

Let's examine these "stages" more carefully.

SCRIBBLE WRITING

When children first begin to use crayons and pencils, they are excited and enthusiastic because they find a new way to express themselves. They quickly learn that some things they "draw" (or "write") can be understood by others. This new way to communicate is ready for their use in storytelling. Children will scribble story after story, and will be encouraged in this early phase merely by being allowed to read their scribble stories to an audience. During the child's exploration of this method of communication (in the early kindergarten and first grade, possibly), the child is concerned with telling or sharing his ideas, and is naturally not bound by the rules of grammar and punctuation that can later become problems. His scribble story can be a definite first step toward the development of positive attitudes and feelings about writing at a later level.

PICTURE WRITING

As a child develops motor control, his use of crayons, paints, and pencil will contribute to a next phase of story writing. All children are capable of telling stories about pictures they have created and are eager to do so. They are often eager to make a picture representation of a story or an event from their experience. (See Chapter IV, "Techniques.") Children from grade one through grade six vary only in level of ability to tell stories, draw inferences, etc., from pictures they have seen or made. This technique is very useful in giving children further opportunity to put their ideas together in a meaningful form—that of a story.

FIRST WORD STORIES

Children, while they experience scribble and picture "writing," are simultaneously learning the forms and sounds of the letters of the alphabet. Some are beginning to recognize words and phrases even to a point where they can use them in writing some basic ideas. Some very early uses for their writing include the naming of persons, places, and things, giving directions how to do or make something, making written announcements, and contributing to group writings.

Many children, however, are ready to use fairly complex ideas in writing even though they themselves cannot write words. Perhaps this phase of a child's story-writing development is the most crucial. How can he continue to improve in his usage of original ideas? Must there be a pause in the development of this ability while his spelling and reading (and other related abilities) "catch up"?

DICTATION TO TEACHER

A skillful teacher can recognize this phase of a child's development and do a great deal to help the child continue to improve. By having the child dictate his ideas to a secretary (the teacher), the child has opportunity to see his ideas put on paper in word form. What other dividends can be reaped from this "dictation to teacher" phase? The child will almost always want to read his story to the class. His own personal story is perhaps one of the most meaningful items he can read. And what about vocabulary? By relating the sight vocabulary directly back to the child's speaking vocabulary (that vocabulary around which the child's ideas were found originally), the time taken for dictation provides a great gain for the child.

Figure 3 is a first-grade boy's story that was dictated to a teacher. After seeing his ideas in word form, the child will want to be able to write them by himself. For a slow child, this "dictation to teacher" phase is very important. Many children, of course, will make the transition to writing their own ideas in word form without going through the "dictation to teacher" phase. About all that is needed to keep children writing at this level is the positive encouragement that is needed in any learning situation.

IMITATION AND IDENTIFICATION

As the story-writing abilities continue to develop, a child's writing patterns are affected by the answers to such questions as (1) what can I write about? (2) who shall I write for? and (3) what style of writing should I use? It is at this stage of development that the children are guided most strongly by two types of behavior—imitation and identification.

One must wonder why, when one child begins to use his classmates as "fictional characters," his writing is soon imitated by other class members; others will soon be using classmates as story characters. And when a teacher is used as the central character of a story for the first time, is it natural to expect that many other children will then explore the teacher as beekeeper, bullfighter, grandpappy, mermaid's beau, soldier, general, Indian fighter, bird, beatnik, pilot, or school principal? As children become involved in this very simple pattern of imitation, they are developing in a quite remarkable way. To be able to construct for themselves a secure framework (that which was imitated) within which they can explore and define their own ideas is in itself the creative aspect of growth in which we are interested. It is true that some children will explore less freely, even within a "borrowed" framework, but the range of individual differences provides ample opportunity for growth even when imitating.

Children in similar patterns will learn to identify with the topics and styles that are accepted by other members of the class as well as by the teacher. The acts of identification will appear as levels of achievement, from which the children are then free to explore and interpret by way of the written word.

SELF-EXPRESSION

Only about 10 per cent of students leaving the elementary grades will have developed their abilities to the point where the guiding value is self-expression, or self-approval (see Chapter II). This perception of story writing is perhaps the most mature perception a child, or anyone, can hold, and one would expect a higher percentage of students to achieve it *if* more children had additional opportunities for writing.

By the time a child reaches this stage, he has learned much about his own writing habits and is usually well aware of his stronger interests, so that the selection of topics becomes a matter of personal choice and preference. The child has also discovered the style of writing that he does best (humorous, adventure, mystery, drama-type), and he has likely accepted this style as being worth while and one he will continue to explore. His ability to criticize his own efforts will be increasingly sharpened, to the degree that he will often rewrite part of a story just to make it "fit" better. Also, he is likely to accept his efforts for the moment, but in future times will learn to look back and make suggestions about how he might have done a "better job."

Also important in this achievement is that as he accepts his own personal style of writing as being adequate for himself—at this moment—he is also learning to respect the efforts of others for the same reason. From the more mature child, only constructive criticism is likely to come. (See Figure 3.)

It was a lovely summer day. The grass was as green as ever; the leaves were swaying with the cool summer breeze. The sky was as blue as the ocean, with clouds that looked as fluffy as cotton. The air was as quiet as if there wasn't anyone else on the world but you. The daisys wer as beautiful as ever before; and even thier smell was like fragrent perfume. Now, wouldn't this paper burn nicely?

It was a lovely summer day. The grass was actually GREEN! The leaves were falling of the tree, like hair off a bald man. The sky was as blue as I am when it's raining. With clouds that looked like fluffy marshmellows. The air was as noisy, as if all the hamburger factorys in the world got together. The weed's were as beautiful as ever; and even there smell smelled like burning rubber. This paper would start a fire nicely too, wouldn't it? H

FIGURE 3

Two Aspects of Programming

A HIT-AND-MISS PROGRAM

Often, however, the kind of writing experiences that positively affect a child's writing abilities are not continuous in an elementary school, and can be attributed only to the teacher who is aware of a child's story-writing needs and of the possibilities for learning in story-writing activities.

Consider now the child who reaches grade five without any previous writing experiences. What additional problems does this child face? Following is a detailed account of an experience with a boy whose previous writing experiences included no opportunity for story writing.

E., a boy of ten, had deep interests in science and phases of mathematics. His reading patterns generally followed these two interests, and he could read with good understanding books on Madame Curie, Louis Pasteur, and other scientists, aspects of anthropology, etc. He was very sensitive to the feelings of others. E. easily had the ideas, interests, and ability to write well. His main problem was seen to involve acknowledging his past experiences with writing, then discovering what standards he was setting for his own writing and observing any conflict between the two. He acknowledged no past experiences. He also observed that his standards for things written were probably the results of his only experience with written stories—the stories of professional writers. He had strong desire to resolve the conflict. After two months of producing unsatisfying products, I suggested that E. freely dictate to me from whatever thoughts came to him. We did this twice, and after each session we looked at the relationship between his ideas as he had "talked" them. E. discovered that he could relate ideas in story fashion. With this positive attitude toward his own ability to narrate, E. came to me before Christmas vacation, saying, "I'm going to forget about my standards and just write. I'll have something for you after vacation." During the next few months E.'s freedom to experience through writing increased, and as he practiced telling stories, so did his ability.

This incident suggests several things. First, it suggests that children must engage in writing experiences continuously if their writing skills and their "standards for writing" are to remain the same. Second, the incident suggests that when a lapse in experience exists—say, a year or more—the standards a child will set for himself will be influenced not by his own ability but by such outside factors as teacher judgment, patterns of professional writers, and others that probably are not realistic for the child's abilities. Third, that the role of self-criticism is important in a child's learning is evident in all areas of school. When a child can actively criticize his own performance, be it writing or arithmetic, this is an act of learning. A child who has opportunity from the beginning stages of development to criticize his own progress will continue to grow and to learn. He must, however, criticize from standards that are realistic to his level of performance, or the "progress" will likely result in negative attitudes and feelings of defeat or inadequacy, even dislike for story writing.

Now that teachers everywhere are trying to adapt the local curriculum to individual differences, more opportunities for story writing are being given to children. Story writing by its very nature is an individually satisfying experience. The child explores ideas and thoughts at his own level of insight and thinking. He relates into story form experiences from his own background. He often uses his own interest areas as the setting for his stories. Because writing is done more slowly than speaking, the child often discovers relationships unique to his own experiences as he thinks, recalls, infers, etc.

INDIVIDUALIZING EXPERIENCES: A SOURCE
OF MOTIVATION

Teachers will do well to let children explore, at their own levels, their best word usage, operational spelling habits, and sense of language structure. What better place is there to teach than at the levels at which children are ready to learn? One girl, a fifth-grader, rushed up to the teacher and said, "I don't want to stop this sentence, I just sort of want to pause. Should I use a period?" Time was immediately taken by the whole class to discuss the girl's problem. The comma, the colon, the semicolon, and the dash were discussed as to proper usage. Excitement and enthusiasm dominated the learning experience, made meaningful by the actual need for such a discussion.

There it was, shining in the
golden sunshine. It was the prettiest
sight I had ever seen. It was handed down
from my father's father's father—our
BEAUTIFUL GARBAGE CAN!!

CHAPTER IV

TECHNIQUES FOR GUIDING THE DEVELOPMENT OF CHILDREN'S CREATIVE WRITING ABILITIES

PERHAPS the most crucial aspect of classroom operation which contributes to child growth is the type of experience that the teacher provides for the children. The writer is indebted to classroom teachers both from the public schools and from the campus schools of Ohio State University, Arizona State University, and Kutztown State Teachers College in Pennsylvania for contributions pertinent to the topic Technique.

A "technique," as considered here, will be *an expert method used in accomplishing something, especially in the creative arts.*

We shall first discuss the relationship between oral and written language activities. Then, with the above definition in mind, the writer will deal with several aspects of techniques found to be most effective in the development of children's story-writing abilities: (1) a description of the technique, (2) ideas as to how the technique can be used, (3) when, if beneficial, a sequence of techniques can be utilized, and (4) some comments about introductory language to be used in presenting the technique.

Oral and Written Technique

The most effective development of story-writing abilities cannot be achieved by written practices alone. The reasons are obvious. (1) Because a child relies on verbal speech patterns in communicating during his earlier years, his speaking vocabulary develops first and most rapidly. Not to make use of this present vocabulary would be to miss a great opportunity. (2) Because written practices involve (*a*) speaking, even if silent and to oneself, (*b*) thinking, of organization and pertinent aspects of letter formation, and (*c*) *then* writing the ideas on paper, a teacher must seek other beneficial ways to aid in the development of attitudes and skills crucial to story writing while these elements of writing are being practiced and explored.

Thus it appears that certain oral techniques can provide opportunity for growth, especially during the gap between entering school and beginning to write. (See Figure 4.)

Havighurst, in his *Developmental Tasks and Education,* quotes: "Between the ages of twelve and eighteen months the great moment of speech arrives. . . . At this stage, the child has got (1) the central idea of language—that a word stands for something—and also (2) his own repertory of sounds to draw from in fashioning words."

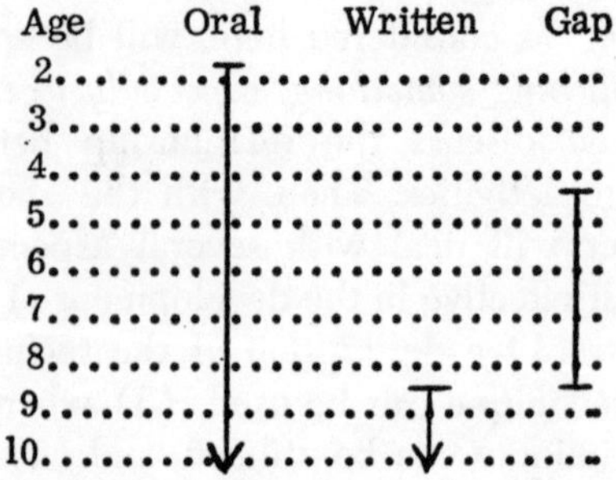

FIGURE 4. An Experience Gap

Among the suggestions that are offered as aids in the development of oral storytelling abilities are (1) to encourage children to tell their own stories, (2) to encourage them to tell stories they have heard from others, (3) to propose a topic, then have some child tell all he knows about it, (4) to begin a story orally, and let the children one at a time contribute as they feel they can relate to its continuity, (5) to let one of them begin a story, then pass it along to a volunteer teller, and (6) to let them set up topics a day in advance to think about and then to tell about in a coming session.

All these things can contribute to their early storytelling successes. More detailed forms of some of these aids will be discussed under such technique headings as Writing From Assigned Topics, Surprise Endings, and Spontaneous Speaking.

Techniques for Teaching

SCRIBBLE WRITING

When children first come to school, they are fascinated with the ways in which crayons and pencils are used. At first, they "write" only in experimentation, moving the crayon this way, then that way. Soon, however, they attach more than personal meaning to their symbols; they begin to make symbols that will have meaning to others as well as themselves. In their first efforts at communication, verbal accompaniment is usually needed for clarity's sake. It is during this period that children can begin to write stories through their kind of scribble writing.

Children are ready to tell stories verbally. They will be eager to scribble-write their stories on paper to share with the class later in a storytelling session. Having opportunity to write and tell stories at this age (kindergarten and first grade) will have a positive effect on their attitudes toward writing stories in the future.

The teacher can often suggest a general idea for them to scribble-write about, but the children should be encouraged to decide upon their own ideas as much as possible. They usually choose an idea that they are quite familiar with, and thus will be able to talk about it with personal interest and from experience. The variety of interests chosen, even at this early age, will result in a sharing session that is both interesting and educational to the listeners.

PICTURE WRITING

An activity closely associated with the scribble-writing stage—and often accompanying that stage—is picture writing. Children may use this type of story writing in several ways: (1) they may make a picture to tell a certain story; (2) they may make a picture to tell about only one event or part of a story they have heard; (3) they may develop a story about any picture they have made. This higher relationship between picture "writing" and storytelling is indicated by both the increased control of symbols and the increased amount of planning necessary to tell or write "certain things."

Children will often get their ideas for story writing from units or general subjects being covered by the class. The writer recalls a group of third-graders who were having one of their first flings at writing ideas. This group, at the time studying how farmers help people in the city, were interested in the numerous people who make money from the farm products. (E.g., milk goes from the cow to the farmer to the dairy to the consumer.) One child thought how nice it would be to get milk straight from the cow, and thus eliminate many of the middle moneymakers. The theme of his drawing and story was "Straight from the cow to you." Others adopted a similar theme while using such products as eggs, beef, and pork.

Children will begin making pictures to tell stories as early as grade one. Again, individual themes will permit exciting exploration of this communication form. The development of relationships between pictures and stories will contribute to many later learning tasks. For instance, in reading much stress is placed upon the ability to read pictures. In social studies and science, children are often asked to draw inferences from related pictures or to clarify word meanings from observing pictured objects and events.

Specific suggestions for implementing this picture-writing technique:

> Display each picture for at least a day; have class discuss descriptive words; then write the story told by the picture.
>
> Present a panel or comic strip; have the children write the story.
>
> Make a picture to convey an idea.
>
> Make a mural to convey a story or event.
>
> Make cartoons, single or in series, to portray a story or an idea.

SPONTANEOUS SPEAKING

One of two types of speaking that provide opportunities for on-the-spot imagining and thinking is the technique of speaking spontaneously. Either the teacher or the class makes up the topics to be used as a chance pool to be drawn from. Then as each speaker draws his chance topic, he begins to speak for a designated period of time. Generally, the lower the grade is, the shorter should be the time limit. To speak spontaneously for thirty seconds on one topic can be a real challenge to a third-grader, while as much as a minute and a half can be used effectively by fifth- and sixth-graders who have had experience with spontaneous speaking. Designation of time interval is based mainly upon (1) the child's repertoire of general facts and (2) his familiarity with verbal-association techniques. With repeated experiences, perhaps three or four times a year, the children will improve markedly in their apparent ease in speaking.

With this technique, as in the next, the relationship to writing is a direct one. Children must have opportunity to relate ideas to one another; and if this is done verbally at first, the concept of storytelling will develop more easily. Children who have not had direct experiences in speaking (and opportunity to relate ideas verbally) will likely have a more difficult time when beginning to write because of the other jobs that also appear—punctuation, spelling, sentence structure, and others that are often the prime concern of teachers.

Specific suggestions for implementing the technique of spontaneous speaking:

> The teacher can first prepare topics, such as cars, bridges, pets, baseball, arithmetic, or any noun that the children would be familiar with.
> The children can learn to suggest topics that are meaningful.

EXTEMPORANEOUS SPEAKING

Several teachers have suggested a speaking activity similar to extemporaneous speech. One name given to the technique is stream of thought; another name suggested is free talking from a given topic. Generally the child begins from a chance topic or subject, then is allowed freedom to move from topic to related topic in free association. To structure the speech by telling at least two things about each of the related topics before going on to a new association is an advanced use of this technique.

Extemporaneous speaking can accompany the introduction of almost any activity that entertains the idea of a "topic." To use the technique in the third grade is not too early because by this time many children are giving reports and having discussions of chosen topics.

The technique of speaking extemporaneously gives the child opportunity (1) to be imaginative on the spot, (2) to relate topics from his own understanding, (3) to have fun with ideas in the free-association setting, and these things while (4) speaking from an assigned or chosen topic. The technique can be used as a language task, a game, or to introduce a kind of writing —depending on the needs of the class and the interpretation of the teacher.

This technique differs from spontaneous speaking in that children are allowed to practice free association, and for longer periods of time. It also differs in that children have the chance to relate from one content field to another, and they usually recognize quickly the many possibilities for ideas to speak about. This recognition will be very useful when they are writing, during which they will need a fluency of ideas.

Specific suggestions for implementing the technique of extemporaneous speaking:

> Teacher-made topics, such as mustard, trees, pets, trips, stars, or any noun can be used.
>
> Children can learn to suggest topics to be used.

WRITING ENDINGS TO ORAL OR WRITTEN STORIES

Much has been inferred about the contributions that oral activities can make to the development of a child's writing patterns. Now, when teachers have taken advantage of the child's speaking vocabulary through the available oral storytelling and speaking activities, how do we then provide for the transition to story writing?

Actually, the child first "wrote" at the stage of scribble writing, if he was given opportunity. And through pictures he continued a form of writing. Now, as his writing vocabulary develops, he may begin to use words to aid him in expressing his ideas.

One of the better aids in this transition from telling to writing is the "unfinished story" technique. In its first use, possibly as early as the latter part of the first grade with some groups, the teacher tells the plot of a short story, then has each child add in his own way what seems to be a good ending for the story. Some children may prefer to do their ending in picture form rather than word form at first. By late second grade most children will have made the transition to the written ending.

An advancement from this stage is to have one child, or even several children, tell the introduction and body of a story; then make each class member responsible for his appropriate ending.

Another use of this technique is for the teacher to provide the children with a written but unfinished story. The children will read the story before making their own intepretations of an appropriate ending for it.

Specific suggestions for implementing the technique of writing endings to unfinished stories:

> The teacher supplies the first line of a poem; the children finish it.
>
> The teacher supplies the first part of story; the children finish it.
>
> A loose-structured plot or list of characters and situations to be used, allowing the children to develop them in their own way.

WRITING GROUP STORIES

In many kindergartens and first grades, children experience further writing patterns through participating in writing group stories. This transition activity from the oral to the written story is very exciting and meaningful for children. By having a chance to dictate to the teacher (who will likely be recorder either at the blackboard or on some other visual surface), each child has the opportunity to say his ideas in a fitting way. True, some children are not ready to make many contributions, but the experience of watching the others in action is basic to their own thinking and will contribute much to their own thinking patterns.

By the latter part of grade two, and easily in grades three and four, some children will get together to write their own group stories. In this phase of growth, groups of two, three, and possibly four will work on a short play or story for several days at a time. Full-length stories and plays (even musicals) will be handled by both class-size and smaller groups during grades five and six. All children should have opportunity to participate in group storytelling, but especially those children who are not ready to undertake writing responsibilities by themselves.

As in other curricular areas, whenever common problems in

writing are met, some students will feel more free to contribute to the group efforts than will others.

Specific suggestions for implementing the technique of group stories:

Writing seasonal poems, stories.

Development of group plays, followed by individual plays written along similar patterns and used in the group effort.

Plays based on television, texts, other plays, etc.

WRITING FROM ASSIGNED TOPICS

Apparently one of the more common techniques used by public-school teachers today is writing from assigned topics. Teachers often make use of the holidays, seasons, current events, etc., to engage the children in personal writing. To watch a child interpret Christmas from year to year would be quite educational —if we would do so. A vacation experience and the oft-used autobiography are two other topics widely exploited. (For other results of questionnaires, see the suggested list of topics immediately following this discussion.)

Writing freely from an assigned topic certainly has a place in the list of techniques helpful in promoting writing abilities. It offers chance for organizing and imagining just as much as do the other suggested techniques. Several difficulties in using this technique, however, are (1) that children, not having opportunities for research before writing, often have no background for some of the topics assigned to them; (2) that children more often lack interest in the topics assigned to them; and (3) that children, if allowed to have some choice concerning their topic, will possibly be much more imaginative than teachers are around Christmas time.

This technique is especially useful in such related study areas as history, social studies, and science. Interpreting, drawing relationships, and making comparisons and contrasts along with other tasks can be achieved through written assignments. In this instance, research materials are available, and the child's awareness of related content can be bolstered by them.

Specific suggestions for implementing the technique of writing from assigned topics are—

Using such titles as—
Why frogs have bulging eyes.
Why a rabbit has a cottontail.
What would happen if pills were developed that would substitute for food?
or if everyone always told the truth about everything?
Writing tall tales about a certain event or character.
Subjective: My Three Wishes.
Imaginary
The Day I Landed on Mars.
My Kingdom in the Sea.
Use of first person—such as "When I first looked upon the scene, I was terrified!"
Brainstorming (used here as imagination): The School of the Future.
"Definite need" stories
for school newspaper.
for various contests.
for city newspaper.
Current events: If I were president.
What I would do if I were elected dog-catcher.
Music appreciation: What Stephen Foster liked as a boy.
Autobiographies.
Riddles, jokes, rhymes, jingles, directions.
Cards for special days.

WRITING DESCRIPTION

During a child's early attempts at writing, he is likely to rely heavily on words that show (1) actions and (2) who or what performed the action. Description, even though the child describes well verbally, will follow this basic thought pattern in most cases.

Some children, especially the more sensitive ones, are likely to develop rapidly and without as much encouragement to a high level of descriptive writing. These children will provide incentive for others to try to describe a set condition such as how the sky appears, what I feel like, how the wind sounds. A discussion of words, and the special feelings some words seem to relate, is a good technique to use at this time. Perhaps the class as a whole will discuss a setting and could list appropriate descriptive words on the blackboard. Then using some of their words, each child begins to pen the relationships that exist for his feelings and the setting. Generally, the lower the grade, the more the situation should be structured with group word lists, etc. Older children will adapt quickly to the use of description, and this attitude will carry over into their other writing activities.

To describe something that has a special personal meaning is one of the most important forms of self-expression; thus, except when helping children to become familiar with the concept, much of their descriptive writing should be of a personal flavor.

Specific suggestions for implementing the technique of descriptive writing are—

Expressing dreams, sensations, feelings, sounds, observations of nature and seasons.

BATHOS

Bathos is a writing technique that builds up an idea or an event, then with a single comment tears the positive feeling apart. A dictionary definition states that bathos is "a ridiculous descent from the lofty to the commonplace in discourse." The technique is used when the writer tries to build up feeling and emotion for the idea or event, then with the ironical twist tries to shatter that feeling or emotion. Supposedly, the more an idea can be built up —or the more positively one can be led to think of something— then also the more effectively can bathos be used to bring the idea back to reality. A use of subjective description followed by objective ridicule can also describe the technique.

Children are most normally exposed to writings and stories that have happy endings . . . or at least have a positive moral conclusion. The written use of bathos enables the writer to add much color and richness to his story. The humorous touch is added with the ironical twist of the writer's insight. Children can learn quickly and easily to use bathos in dealing with elements of their daily experience. For purpose of further immediate discussion, John's example follows:

There it was, standing tall and shining in the sunshine. It was the prettiest sight I have ever seen. It was handed down from my father's father's father—our beautiful garbage can.

This technique is natural for following the normal happy ending. The child can now explore many experiences, trying to see these experiences from at least two points of view, ideally and ironically.

When the teacher introduced this technique to his sixth-grade class, he began by having the class answer the question "What do you think a story's ending should be like?" The class listed such descriptions as happy, having everything turn out right, having all the problems solved. The teacher then suggested that up to that time almost all the stories they had written had been ended in one of those ways. However, was it possible to build up the story so that the reader or listener would be expecting a "good" ending, then to slash down all the good feeling with a single comment? Needless to say, many of the children adapted this technique to their own style and used it in many of their personal stories thereafter.

SURPRISE ENDINGS

Bathos is an excellent introduction to the story with a surprise ending. Whereas bathos deals normally only with one idea or one event, the surprise ending follows a full-length story combining action, description, personal feelings and insights, and other elements of storytelling used by a child.

After a child has used the technique of bathos in its more simple setting, he is quite often able to relate the surprise ending quickly to a more complex setting.

Instructional guidance in the use of this technique is mainly one of helping the children to see the relationships of bathos (recommended as a previously learned technique) and the more complex surprise ending. As children adapt the surprise element to their writing, they will likely use it not only at the end but at the beginning or nearer the middle of their stories.

FROM MY WINDOW

Paul H.
Fifth Grade

I look too the sky and what do I see?
Clouds, as light as light can be.

I look too the ground and what do I see?
A rabbit, dancing so merily.

I look up and through the air,
A bird sings, just over there.

I look and I look and something says to me,
Where do these things come from, here to be?

I wonder I wonder as I look o'r the sea,
Who, yes who brings these things to me?

And then comes a feeling from deep down inside,
Something on which I seem to ride.

Yes now I know who brings us such fun
He in heaven, God, he's the one.

CHAPTER V

CHARACTERISTICS OF A CREATIVE WRITING ATMOSPHERE AT ELEMENTARY LEVELS

WHAT are the important characteristics of a classroom atmosphere than can best guide children in their attempts at creative expression? What is the teacher's role in that "writing" atmosphere?

At least six important characteristics of a creative writing program can be readily discerned. They are (1) a very basic *time allowance* in a child's day when he has opportunities to participate in the essential experiences of a writing program, (2) *positive teacher attitudes* guiding certain aspects of the activity, (3) teacher willingness to be a *source of ideas,* (4) teacher awareness of some effective techniques useful in *guiding children to better writing patterns,* (5) *evaluation* of children's writings, and (6) various *relationships existing between the writing program and other areas* of achievement.

Allowing Adequate Time

"Practice makes perfect" certainly has its implications for phases of the school curriculum. Thus it makes sense to say that if children are to become skilled in writing, they must first be given opportunities to write.

Another activity associated with writing at the elementary levels is a sharing of what one has written. This sharing activity usually provides the main incentive that encourages children to explore their use of written words in expressing their ideas. The time for sharing also enables the class member to listen to efforts similar to his own, and to have his first chance to become a critic of writing patterns—thereby having a chance to strengthen aspects of his own written work.

Providing time for children to write, then to share, can—under effective guidance—give opportunities for satisfying many objectives of the total language program. The children will have real needs to use various punctuation marks and capital letters for different purposes. Also, a consciousness of good spelling habits is further developed when children write for personal purposes. However, though the total language program is benefited in many ways, perhaps the most important goal to be realized during this time for personal writing is the individual's ability to develop ideas that satisfy his purposes of self-expression.

Because children's writing habits are often closely related to their interests—and thus their reading patterns—an increasingly common scheduling practice has been to have a "reading *or* writing" time included as part of the total language program. The time allowed in most class situations for personal writing experiences depends mainly upon two influences; one is the emphasis of the total curriculum, and the second is the teacher's attitudes toward child growth in this area.

Teacher Attitudes

Needless to say, a teacher's attitudes are important influences in all areas of a child's growth. When a teacher speaks positively of something, that something can take on new importance to a listener or learner. Often when a teacher can show eagerness for an area of study, the students also exhibit added interest in that area.

In connection with writing, the most important positive attitudes that a teacher should exhibit when guiding children are, first, that the child has opportunity to express his ideas in *his own* way, using *his* vocabulary on *his* level of thinking and expression; second, that the child by writing often will show growth just as in other needful areas; and third, that a child can often rely heavily on the incentive that what he writes can be shared with his classmates. With beginning writers this idea of sharing is very significant, and it often is the most important value guiding their efforts as they write.

Not only should a teacher encourage writing to take place freely, but there seem to be certain growth patterns that a teacher can be aware of in recognizing a child's progress. Children have their own sets of values—which, when recognized as guidelines to their efforts, give at least some indication of their maturing. For instance, it seems that at least three differing purposes for writing guide their efforts from grades one through six. In the very early part of this period, children will often "write for writing's sake" as they are first fascinated by the way they can use symbols, pictures, and even scribbling to tell their stories. Teachers can add a great deal to these early experiences by finding an occasional period when children can "dictate their stories" to the teacher. These stories are then near-perfect materials that can be used in conjunction with the reading program as well as the writing and sharing program.

Then, during the next levels of development—possibly grades three, four, and five—the child's value seems to become not of "writing for writing's sake" but of writing for peer approval. This value is sometimes a limiting factor upon the efforts of the more sensitive child, but the value provides a stimulus for almost every other child during this period of growth. Kinds of writings that are produced during these years will usually indicate definite interest and reading patterns because the children produce from these elements of their background more freely.

Perhaps the highest level of maturity to be noticed in the elementary levels is illustrated by the child who begins to write to express his ideas in his own way, no other strings attached. It has been the writer's experience that such maturity will occur with no more than three or four out of every thirty children passing the sixth-grade level. However, for these three or four, writing has already become a powerful tool of their imaginations and experience.

One boy, as a fifth-grader, wrote an extremely well-organized science-fiction novel 170 pages long. As a sixth-grader he added a novel of 65 pages to his already long list of writings. Most sixth-graders, however, still consider as highly important the value of sharing for peer approval.

Perhaps a third main area of teacher concern is the way in which this kind of personal writing can lead directly to the satisfaction of individual differences. Here is an area in which children are not even expected, much less wanted, to be alike in their efforts. Individual styles should be encouraged, and will vary widely as children begin to express themselves according to their changing moods and different backgrounds. The amounts of writing done will vary too as each child is encouraged to contribute to the maximum of his ability.

The Teacher as a Source of Ideas

Should the teacher provide topics to write on? How much help should she give? When?

The teacher's role as a source of ideas is quite well defined by the make-up of each class she works with. The stronger writers can almost always define their own topics, ideas, stories, etc. But when a teacher is needed by any child to supply an idea, the most effective idea for that child will be one that opens a passageway to his own experiences and interests. Children are highly dependent upon their individual backgrounds for the content that they can readily use in their writings. Therefore, the teacher's most effective approach is to help them tap their own resources by suggesting ideas that in a fullest sense are meaningful to them.

The Teacher's Role in Guiding Children
to Better Writing Patterns

As children are open to testing their skills through writing, how can the teacher effectively aid the child in increasing his ability to write?

Teachers who recognize the strong relationship between reading and writing patterns can greatly influence individual growth in writing. Debbie, as a sixth-grader, was interested in stories with surprise endings. As suggested by the teacher, she read several short stories by both Poe and O. Henry.

Children can also learn from discussion of a specific writer's style. Often they will recognize a characteristic of a style that is particularly effective in "setting a mood," and this recognition can carry over into a child's writing.

Many other language experiences are helpful in enabling a child to express himself through writing. Here are some sample techniques believed helpful:

1. Children are eager to speak spontaneously, and one way to use this technique is to write various topics on pieces of paper to be "drawn" and then "spoken about" for a limited time (perhaps beginning with 30 seconds and increasing to 1½ minutes over three or four sessions).

2. Another oral technique that becomes a favorite is extemporaneous speech. A specific use of this style is to have a child say at least two things about a subject before changing to a related subject. Time limits can also be adjusted to their familiarity with the technique.

3. A third oral device, one often used, can be called group story telling. Children enjoy beginning a story, and taking over the storytelling and crucial points, to be later relayed to another teller for the ending. It helps the children when the mood or style of the story can be set before their interpretation.

4. The unfinished-story technique, where all writers operate

from a common basis of thinking, is also a useful one. Often the teacher can provide the setting, characters (if any), and situation involved, and the children can add their personal endings based upon their backgrounds for thinking and abilities to express themselves.

Evaluation

When is a child's creative writing to be considered "good" or "bad?" Which standards shall be considered when judging a child's written efforts?

Generally, teachers recognize that possible answers to these questions must be related to the specific purposes for which writing takes place. Further, more and more teachers are recognizing that the most valid *purpose* behind the creative writing program is that of fostering as much individual growth as is possible—not that of comparing students with other students!

With the goal of fostering individual growth setting the direction for our programs, we can readily see some of the implications which must guide the evaluation of children's creative writing efforts.

First, the individual child's purposes for writing are constantly changing as his experience, his reading patterns, and his attitudes are growing and expanding. Thus our task becomes one of using his changing or "growing" purposes as a basis for evaluating his written thoughts. For example, a second-grade child will usually have little contact with such marks of punctuation as the colon or the semicolon. To evaluate that child's first efforts with such meaningless standards would be indeed an injustice. However, a fourth- or fifth-grader who has questioned the use of such pause-making devices will have incorporated their use into his own standards of what good writing is, and will expect to be guided toward the type of writing of which he is capable.

Second, emphasis should be placed upon the child's evaluation of his own efforts. When a child judges himself, he is more likely to be aware of his weaknesses and strengths. As he critically surmises his efforts, he will sense whether or not they are his best, and even if improvement has been made. Children learn to evaluate themselves according to their own standards quickly and with more objectivity. Have you ever allowed children to set up rules for a game, then listened to them discuss the violations that have posed threats to the group rules? If we are trying to foster the child's ability to evaluate his abilities, then certainly creative writing sessions offer us opportunity galore.

A third guideline for evaluating children's writings is the class or group purpose which the writing is often intended to satisfy. For instance, in getting things ready for publication in a class newspaper or a class collection of writings, the jobs of editing and re-editing may follow certain restrictions and limitations that have been set up by the group. In these instances, the individual needs to be aware of the group's standards as well as his own; and if he is, the evaluation should be according to the most important standards he is to strive towards.

Two other guidelines for evaluation are closer to process than the three already mentioned. Though each implies values and standards, both also give direction to possible procedures and techniques for use in the process of evaluating.

First, the teacher who is trying to provide for maximum individual growth will offer *encouragement* (recognizing that the child is working on *his* level) and reinforcement concerning any efforts the child can make. In reinforcing a child's efforts to succeed, emphasis should be directed toward (1) any growth that has already taken place, and (2) possible chances for growth in the future. Some examples follow.

RELATED TO 1. When a child does such a simple thing as making an effort to write description—say, of clouds—whatever the child writes usually represents at least his own ideas, feelings, and ability to use words. The teacher can reinforce his concept of the sky by merely acknowledging his right to see it that way, although much more effective reinforcement would occur if the teacher says something like this: "Oh, I *like* the way you used *that* word," or "*That's* an interesting way to describe clouds." If we remember that we should evaluate their writings according to standards for children, opportunities for positive reinforcement come often.

IN DIRECTION 2. Pointing out chances for future growth, we

have a chance to supplement the child's direction with our own technical insight. We might, for instance, say to a child, "Your last story was a very interesting one. Now, would you like to know how to make it even a little *more* interesting?" Then we can proceed to give any direction that the child is ready to handle that will improve both his standards for writing and his performance in the various activities of the program.

A second implication for process makes use of the writing standards professed by each member of the class. When a child writes, he often likes to share his written materials with other members of the class. After sharing, the teacher can ask, "Class, how do you think Tommy has improved his story today?" or "How did Tommy make his story an exciting one to listen to?" You will notice that both of these questions direct the children to make *constructive* criticism of Tommy's efforts. The children will be thinking critically about Tommy's writing from their own standards of what writing is, but will be asked only for aspects of Tommy's improvement. As each child thinks critically about what good writing is, and about how the writings of other children are being improved, the standards and performances of those children who are doing the critical thinking will be guided and enhanced in directions that are more or less "tried and proven." Confidence building, or reinforcement, is thus occurring as these children think critically of writing patterns, styles, topics, and other aspects of the activity. The use of group standards and the individual standards within the group can thus be used to reinforce each other.

Relationship of Writing to Other Areas

Certainly creative writing can be taught no more than art; but it can be taught as much. If creative writing is, in fact, an ability, then it can also be taught as much as the skill of reading or the skill of computation can be taught.

More than a separate skill, however, the ability to write creatively must be thought of as a combination of various skills contributing to productivity in a unique direction. For the influences upon a child's writing patterns are many, and include (1) reading patterns and interests, (2) grammatical usage, (3) spelling, (4) other curricular areas demanding conceptual patterns, such as science, social studies, and arithmetic, and (5) any area, such as art or music, in which individual expression is emphasized.

How is the child's development in creative writing likely to be affected? What is the character of specific relationships between creative writing and each of the influences listed above?

READING

The reading patterns of a child include (1) type of materials read, (2) amount of materials read, (3) breadth of materials read, and (4) the role of various reading materials in a child's total experience background. Each of these patterns, or all of them, may affect the development of writing patterns.

For instance, as a child advances through certain stages of social growth, the type of material that is preferred for a child's free-reading program changes. Boys in fifth and sixth grades are generally much more interested in big-time athletics and historical events than are boys at an earlier age. Thus the boy's background will include more know-how concerning athletics, and more experiences with actual athletic events. Both know-how and actual experience will often come out in a boy's stories. In the same manner, girls of this age will often write stories about horses—a very popular reading interest for girls ten to twelve years of age.

It is possible to have the same "reading experience" several times. When boys read *only* about animals, their background (from which their ideas for writing will come) will tend to be more limited than if animals are only one of many reading interests. Children search for the limits of their imagination, and at the other end of this extreme is this example.

A fifth-grade boy was searching for an idea for a new story. As fifth-graders go, this boy was a prolific writer—having already written one 95-page science-fiction book that was published. The teacher, knowing something of his many experiences in the family's Rocky Mountain cabin, suggested that the boy use the mountains as a setting for his new effort. The boy replied that he didn't want to use his experiences for this story because "they set limits" on his imagination. He wanted to be completely free from the limits his experiences sometimes posed. The topic he eventually chose was concerned with mental telepathy and the implications this process might have for the people in his mystery!

Most children, however, need to depend upon their previous experiences (including reading) for ideas and relationships to present in story form.

This suggests the role that *reading in breadth* can play when a child attempts to create through written expression. Generally, the wider the background experiences of the child, the more free will he be to try his writing techniques out in a variety of settings. The child with a wide background of experiences can thus improve on certain aspects of techniques while maintaining a high interest level in writing his thoughts creatively.

A child who reads constantly will be largely dependent upon his reading background when drawing forth material to write about. In contrast, a child who is more observant in actual behavior situations, and who reads little, will not depend on, or be restricted by, his reading habits. Those children who do read constantly, however, will normally depend so much upon their reading for their personal stories that much imitation will take place. Imitation in this sense need not be a negative act, as long as the child is organizing the events or happenings in his own way. In fact, some successful experience with imitation and organizing in this way is often necessary for the future release of more personal and creative works. If a child continues to move away from imitation as his technique, he is most certainly progressing in his writing independence.

A child will use his reading as a very vital source of ideas. Though research is not available, it appears that better and more varied reading experience will contribute to more profitable writing experience for children.

Reading is often related to writing in at least two other ways. First, when a child writes a story, a poem, a notice, or any other type of material, this written piece can serve as a supplemental reading device when the child reads his own work to the teacher or the class. This technique makes direct usage of his own ideas, vocabulary, and verbal expression—three very important elements of the reading process.

Second, a child will often be stimulated in his writing to *read for ideas or styles* that he can use. For example, when one child had succeeded with the technique of bathos (sudden or surprise twist of thought), it occurred to her that she could construct a full story and use the technique of a surprise ending. This child then read several of O. Henry's short stories before writing a couple of McClung's of her own! (One is "Blood Red," included in Chapter VII, sixth-grade style.)

GRAMMAR

Creative writing contributes to the development of a child's mastery of grammar in two very important ways. First, the various creative writing activities provide a setting in which the child will have opportunity to practice the various grammatical tools, such as punctuation, capitalization, and correct usage. Second, a child in the process of writing will also try out new or different grammatical structures, and he will recognize new needs in his own style or sense of structure.

One child came up to the teacher while writing in the middle of a sentence and asked, "What kind of mark can I use? I don't want to use a period, because I don't want to stop it completely. I just want to make a pause—not a stop." The teacher then got the class into a discussion of the child's problem. The comma, the dash, the colon, and the semicolon were among the pause indicators that were discussed.

SPELLING

The child has several vocabularies: among them are the speaking vocabulary, the writing vocabulary, and the spelling vocabulary, these three being in the supposed order of size, large to small. When a child is free to explore and write from his writing vocabulary, he is sure to have some difficulty with spelling. However, if he is not free to use words outside of his spelling vocabulary, the restriction is not only on the kind of idea that he can construct, but also on the more general denial of his normal style of expression—that style which he uses naturally in every other setting of his life.

Therefore, creative writing experiences are settings in which the child can use both words studied and words not studied. His very use of the "extra" words will promote some interest and efficiency in the spelling of words not on the spelling list. Many teachers are, in fact, structuring their spelling lists *from* the child's actual needs in spelling.

Also emphasis upon idea building rather than spelling is believed to have a more meaningful effect upon the child's later writing patterns. What good will knowing how to spell a word correctly do the child if he cannot then use his words in building ideas?

THINKING PROCESSES

Creative writing is closely related to the kind of thinking that is promoted in science and social studies, where stress is often upon patterns of conceptual development. For instance, psychology indicates that in forming a concept, we go through such processes as discrimination, elimination, and differentiation. What else is a child doing when he is selecting, organizing in both thought and logical sequence, and drawing relationships together by means of the written word? The concepts a child is forming when he is writing a story often present a miniature summary of his best thinking on the subject central to that story. As the child writes, so does he organize his experiences; and often, while he organizes, concepts appear that lead him to new insights and understandings of both his writing patterns and, more generally, himself.

Certainly educators have organized curriculum areas for convenience. Facts, ideas, and concepts that relate well to one another can be handled in a more economical, efficient, and often meaningful way if they are grouped together. However, the main teaching job we hope to accomplish—regardless of the subject-matter area—is helping children to become more effective thinkers and problem solvers.

Thus pertinent aspects of thinking are stressed as important in any learning experience. Those aspects listed below are often clearly evident in a child's written efforts.

1. Making contrasts (citing differences).
2. Making comparisons (citing likenesses).
3. Drawing inferences (theorizing).
4. Noting limitations of data.
5. Drawing conclusions.
6. Noting relationships between existing data.
7. Putting data together (from several areas) to form relationships.
8. Noting the sequence of events.
9. Using vocabulary in varied "meaning" situations.

Not only are these evidences of thinking processes present, but often one or more of them will form the plot or basis for the writing effort.

Summary

At least six aspects of a writing atmosphere have been considered.

1. A time for writing is essential.
2. Positive teacher attitudes should guide individual writing efforts.
3. Writing experiences should be as meaningful as possible.
4. Writing skills can be increased by many other language activities.
5. Evaluation is indispensable.
6. The writing program is related to other academic areas.

Certainly the writing program as viewed here is very closely related to the reading and total language programs. An atmosphere in which creative writing patterns can be nourished is dependent upon these certain basic classroom characteristics.

WHAT DO CLOUDS THINK OF EARTH?

by John T., 5th Grade

This story is about two clouds. They are discussing the earth. One says, "I wish I were out of here—I keep bumping into clouds, and those planes are always flying through me and angels sitting on my back!"

"That's nothing," said the other, "a satellite just zoomed past me and almost blew me into a million pieces, and a peaso bird stuck his crooked bill in me. Let's get the gang together. I see a plane coming and on the side it says 'Spirit of Colorado' it must be that hot rod again; come on fellows and rain for all your worth!"

WHAT THE CLOUDS THINK OF...

by John T., 5th Grade

CHAPTER VI

CREATIVE WRITING: THE DEVELOPMENT OF THINKING PROCESSES

A CHILD writing creatively is experiencing a great deal that can never be evaluated by looking at what he puts on the paper. Any writer must be a thinker; and in writing he must use those elements of thinking processes that contribute to his exploration of ideas. Of course, not all students will think with the same degree of skill—just as in reading or arithmetic, children perform at various skill levels. Some children, for instance, will prefer to use their imaginative forces, and others (and not only the timid) will continue to use much imitation (and will be guided by outside influences).

As all children write, however, they have experiences with certain aspects of the thinking processes. This chapter will deal with some ideas pertinent to (1) conceptual formation, (2) levels of experience, (3) gaining insights into self, (4) organizing and making inferences from personal experience, and (5) motivation and reinforcement, especially as these aspects of thinking relate to the act of writing creatively.

Conceptual Development

A child's thinking ability is characterized mostly by his ability to conceptualize. In a sense, all children are continually developing new concepts, though some children are slower and less capable than others at the task. At least three important aspects of creative writing activities contribute to conceptual formation: (1) the exploration of personal experiences, needs, and desires, (2) the use of personal "subject-matter" background, and (3) the use of imagination in developing a personal concept of writing style.

Writing is done more slowly than speaking or reading. Thus, when a child is engaged in writing, he must often relate his ideas for the story to his own personal experiences, needs, attitudes, or desires. In making this relationship, the child is doing two things that aid in his own conceptual development.

First, he is actively trying for *greater understanding* of his past experience and present insights. Thus as he makes inferences, comparisons, and contrasts relative to his personal experience, he will make many discoveries leading to concepts and generalizations that are completely new to him.

One child, when writing a story about deer and how men hunted them, suddenly wondered if the deer had any ways to "outsmart humans." Her next chapter carried this title: "Two Baby Deer Get Lessons on 'How to Outsmart Humans.'" The concept of deer living purposefully was related through the remainder of the child's written effort.

Second, the writing child is using his past experience as a guideline to his "written experience"; and this condition often leads the child to a *restructuring* of his past experiences. Accompanying insights are often vitally changed, and are seen with much more clarity than his previous interpretations or concepts of his past experiences.

The content background of a child also plays a vital role in his written efforts. Perhaps even more than with personal experience, the child is continually organizing and reorganizing his ideas and knowledge. Through his writing he will make personal discoveries of many relationships between aspects of his content background.

One boy was wondering about a certain scientific phenomenon (why the ocean floor is so salty). Then on a future occasion he was writing about the life of a drop of water. As he related his experiences of "Freshie," he suddenly theorized that the many rivers which emptied into the oceans probably carried the salt there—from the land bodies. This act led to a personal investigation by the child to see if the theory was an acceptable one. The theory does coincide with aspects of current theory.

Levels of Experience

Children operate from three levels of experience when they write. These levels—sensory, symbolic, and inferential—also represent levels of critical thinking abilities. Each of the levels implies a reaction to one's experience, with the level of sensory experience being basic and primary and the level of experience through inference being the most abstract.

The child's best thinking (and his ability to write) will vary from subject to subject on the basis of his "experience level." For instance, a child not knowing the technicalities of earth-sun-moon relationships will most likely be limited to description (based on visual, or sensory, experience) if asked to write about those relationships. However, a child who has studied the relationships of these heavenly bodies can use his symbolic understandings as he writes, and may even be able to infer relationships between other solar bodies on the basis of his symbolic understandings.

As was stated, many children's ideas will be based upon *sensory* experiences—those experiences which they have actively participated in by seeing, hearing, smelling, feeling, or tasting. Description of experiences at this level is likely to be related with confidence and preciseness, as the child's ability to conceptualize at this level is well developed and often practiced.

Normally a child will include much *symbolic* expression and experience in his thinking. Especially is this level characterized by fantasy, humor, and other less realistic styles of writing. One child wrote of 150-proof milk! Another wrote of a peaso bird—symbolic of a teacher. Still another wrote "The Mystery of the Missing Rabbit Hole." The use of concepts symbolic in nature as "central themes" for writing is a most popular choice with writers at any level.

The third aspect of experiences—that of making *inferences* from one's experiences—is often more fun for the child to handle, and will result in such explorations as the "why the giraffe has a long neck" type, or "what I would do if I were——." In another of its popular present uses, many children write science fiction with such projection into the future that will be most rewarding for both writer and listener.

Children usually limit the use of their powers of inference to relating (1) events or (2) causal relationships accompanying events. Occasionally a child will use his insights to human behavior, interpersonal relationships, human feelings, and ways of interpreting as the central theme of his writing.

Self-awareness and Creative Writing

In many ways, creative writing techniques lead to increased self-awareness on the part of the writer. In fact, when a child writes, he necessarily must use *his ideas, his feelings, his sense of relationships,* and *his style of saying them.* As the child thinks about what to write and how to write it, he is making a direct attempt to understand his ideas and feelings—especially as to how they relate to his topic.

Some children develop a strong self-concept as to their personality type. They may then even relate this to their self-made style of writing. One child felt strongly that he could write only more sincere, serious types of things, such as realistic description of actual phenomena or events. These strong feelings conflicted with his ideas of what the class members enjoyed hearing. He wrote a few things anyway, and his more serious descriptions were always a treat for others to hear. He shared his writings with others only when he felt they would like them—which is perfectly normal behavior.

Another child wrote only humorous poems, stories, and jottings, and was quite prone to criticize his own work. Only a few children will be very successful with a large variety of writing styles, as the individual child's personality and way of looking at things will strongly show forth in his writings. Those children who can adapt to many styles successfully are clearly learning to use writing as a tool of expression—and usually will enjoy the exploration of even more styles.

Children can also learn to use writing to satisfy the same purposes for which some of us "blow off steam." They learn to write out their feelings of distress; and as they analyze them enough to write them out, the children are able to put the "trouble spots" into a time or social perspective.

One child, after being verbally spanked by a teacher, went to her pencil-and-paper outlet and wrote:

my true thoughts

I feel like I want to say everything I think. It may not be a nice thing to do but the things I want to say aren't nice either. I am not aloud to cuss so I don't think I will, so how on earth can I say the things I feel. I am about to burst and I feel like I am on fire. I am tense and my nerves are on edge. I am mad, I guess that's the best way to exspress my feelings. As I look around I see that no one is happy but 3 people but still I feel no better. Maybe I'll cool down by the end of the day but I seriously dought it. My eyes seem to be burning and tired. My cold seems to be getting worse and I find myself writing faster. I think I better forget what has happen today but it will be *hard*, but I am going to try *hard*!

The End

Several types of activities (some of which have been mentioned in Chapter IV) which lead directly to newer and deeper self-insights are typified by the following three:

> My best wish, or my three wishes
> My happiest day
> An experience I'll always remember

In other instances, children may recognize strong attitudes and interest recurring in several of their attempts at writing. Often a child will use this recognition as a basis for further understanding—and the recognition can often serve as an incentive to more activity and reading concerning those things discovered.

Organizing Personal Experience

Another aspect of self-perception that characterizes children's writings is concerned with the organization of ideas and feelings into expressive forms. Children put themselves—complete with attitudes, feelings, fears, and obsessions—into their stories with minimum fear of being "seen" by others.

One child, aged twelve, who had just learned that she was an adopted child, projected her own situation into another scene she was very familiar with—the corral full of horses. Her story follows:

SHADOW

It was a dark, rainy morning on the range in Oklahoma. A white mare was slowly nudging a little grey colt to its feet. Upon the hill, not far away, the proud father looked down at his son. His father was a big black—king of the wild horse band. Finally, the mare got the little colt to his feet; he took two steps and clunk, down he went! His mother nudged him up again. This time he took three steps before falling down. Just as he finally began to get somewhere, a black colt, by the name of Smoky, gave him a mard push, and down he went. The mare saw this and immediately chased off the intruder. Then she and her colt settled down.

In the middle of the afternoon, the colt and his mother woke up, and the colt got to his feet, and he and his mother walked off down the pasture. Just then, the black colt came tearing down the other side of the pasture with his grey mother. The grey mare stopped to talk with the colt's mother, and the black one took over the job of teasing the colt. Just then the colt's father climbed the hill, gave a terrifying whinny which sent the whole herd roaring down the canyon. The colt's mother whinnied to her little son to run. Then he saw the most terrifying sight of his life—men with ropes, swinging them high above their heads and catching a horse every time. The herd was still roaring down the canyon, the colt's father in the lead. Faster and faster they went until the colt could no longer see the men. They came across a wide plateau and pretty soon the big black leader slowed the herd. The little colt looked around for his mother, but couldn't find her. He whinnied helplessly. Beside him was the little black colt and his mother, but there was no sign of the colt's own mother. Finally, the old, black leader came silently down the canyon toward the colt. The big black stopped within two feet of the colt. The colt just stared. The big black turned to the grey mare beside him, and whinnied to her softly.

That night the little colt saw the big grey mare coming down the trail. He silently walked over to her, and nudged her gently. The grey turned back up the trail, with the little colt tagging behind. The colt had found a new mother.

Months went by and the little colt grew strong and healthy, but he still remembered that frightful day when his mother was taken from him and his first day in the world. The old black was still king, and the colt still had trouble with Smoky, but still life was enjoyable. By the time the colt was two years old he was as strong as any four horses, and could lick his weight in all the colts.

One afternoon Smoky came across the field to start his teasing again. The colt let him get just close enough and turned on him, hoofs flying. Both horses hit the ground and each other as hard as they were able, but finally, tired and worn, the colt chased Smoky away.

Finally, at the age of three, one morning the colt decided that it was about time for him to leave the herd, so he asked one of the colts to come along with him, and they started out. Half way down the side of a mountain, the young colt saw a sight that stirred old memories. Men with ropes and other horses coming toward the canyon where the herd was. The colt gave one shrill whinny and dashed off in the opposite direction toward the woods and safety. Too late, the horsemen had seen him; a lasso went around his neck. He was pulled short. Two other ropes went securely around his neck and he was taken back with three other horses. The ranch had many terrifying experiences for him. He was put in a corral with three other horses. He thought to himself, "Well this is good enough. Maybe I can get out of this". It was late that afternoon when the colt saw the men coming, again with ropes, and some sort of a harness and a heavy saddle. They tried getting the saddle on him, but it didn't do much good, because the first one that came near him was sent flying. The man's head hit the railing, and he lay still. When the man didn't get up, the other men went over to get him up. They tried and tried, but it was no good. The man was dezd. The colt was a killer. One of the men went into the house and came out with a loaded shotgun—took careful aim, and was about to fire when quick as a flash—the colt was up and over the fence and galloping out toward the plains. This gave the colt a very good idea of what men were like, but he enjoyed seeing them try to catch him. He decided this was a good way to get a band. If he could get away, they could. So late at night the colt galloped down to the nearby ranches as silently as a shadow, opened the corral and let all the horses out. This went on for many months until not one man in the valley could keep a horse more than a night. So they called a meeting to see what they could do. They all sat down in a nearby hotel and began to discuss it. "He's just like a shadow," Bill Lawrence piped up. "Shadow", that's a real good name for him" said Tom Brewster. So "Shadow" he was.

A child's main job is to try to organize the experiences of his own consciousness, of other persons closely associated with him, and of his personal imaginative powers. That a child has opportunity to organize himself, so to speak, is essential. Sessions in creative writing contribute greatly to this important aspect of a child's maturing.

Motivation and Reinforcement

The ability to express one's ideas with at least the confidence that they will be accepted and respected as being personal contributions is important to all learning activity. Psychological research has shown that success in an effort is an incentive to further effort.

Motivation and reinforcement come from two types of sources —outer and inner. Sources of outer motivation and reinforcement include teacher, parent, peer, and books and other aids designed to provoke senses.

Examples of outer motivation include (1) the teacher making assignments, (2) the teacher telling a child that his work is good or improving, (3) a peer telling his mate that he liked his work, and (4) a parent approving of or listening to the child's efforts.

Inner motivation more ideally leads the child to decide upon his own directions (topics and styles are examples), then to become personally either satisfied or dissatisfied with the results of his efforts. Generally it is motivation of the inner type that teachers ultimately try to promote.

Inner and outer types of reinforcement have similar sources, and each has its own implications for child growth and development. The more mature child is the one less dependent upon either outer motivation or outer reinforcement. This child will be more independent of outer stimuli, and his aim will be more directly related to those personal purposes which his common sense tells him are of value both to himself and to the group. Inner motivation and inner reinforcement will guide the more mature child's learning efforts in writing as in other areas of living.

THE CHILDREN SPEAK

Where do you get your ideas for your stories?

> "I can't really say, because I just start writing and as my thoughts get farther along I get new ideas."
>
> ". . . from my head—I have an idea *before* I start writing of what I'm going to write."
>
> ". . . Mostly from something I read."
>
> "I dream my ideas up! And I think of them while daydreaming or looking at pictures of things."
>
> ". . . from comics and movies."
>
> "I look around and if an idea comes to me I write it down for writing about later."
>
> "I think them up from things that have really happened or something that I would like to have happen to me."
>
> ". . . from places I go and things I do."

What are some things that stop you from writing stories?

> "I just seem to run out of ideas."
>
> "Don't have time (Joke!)."
>
> "I have ideas but don't know how to put them down on paper sometimes."
>
> "Sometimes other studies would be more interesting than writing."
>
> "I feel I can't write very good."
>
> "I get good ideas for writing about, but at the wrong time."
>
> "Sometimes I get discouraged when I feel I can't put my ideas into writing."

CHAPTER VII

INDIVIDUAL
WRITING PATTERNS

PERHAPS the most important need in classroom teaching today is to recognize that individual growth patterns are both positive and potential. An evaluative remark used in Chapter V was "You did a good job with that story, Tim. Now would you like some ideas that will help you do an even better job?" Here the emphasis is twofold: (1) an acceptance of the child's efforts and (2) some directions for future personal growth.

Never before has so much interest and research been related to the recognition and guidance of individuals in the classroom. An attempt is made in this section to relate some of the psychology of individual writing patterns to selected writings. The most fascinating and important aspects of a creative writing program are related to the many, many opportunities both for studying the individual child and in allowing for individual growth patterns to be really expressed.

Do individual children differ with respect to need? outlook on life? What makes for success? interests? modes of expression? Perhaps the differences that *are* being expressed constantly account for many of the difficulties that a teacher faces. Though these differences may lead to difficulties, however, more often they are the "heart" of the class, providing stimulation, enthusiasm, and reinforcement for the efforts of children and teacher alike. It is the challenge of all challenges in the classroom that the teacher faces when she tries to provide opportunity for each child to become more self-directive and self-expressive.

Yes, we acknowledge that individuals do differ, and in the pages that follow we shall see how these differences are evident in children's writings. The remainder of this chapter will include a discussion of five individual writing patterns, and will focus on (1) examples of their efforts, (2) various styles and types of writing tried by each, (3) problems peculiar to the child's development, and (4) any incidents pertinent to the materials included.

Whenever possible, the original writings will be presented—complete with emphasis techniques, misspelled words, original punctuation patterns, and other mechanical characteristics. It is possible to notice the development of improved patterns of mechanics almost from one story to the next; however, the emphasis to be studied here is more directly related to the development of ideas and ways of expression. (Stories edited by the students are so indicated throughout the next two chapters.)

Debbie

The first selections come from the pen of Debbie, and were written in her fifth- and sixth-grade years.

Bedtime

Once upon a twilight dreary,
 I was crying, my eyes were teary.
I had to go to bed, no fun,
 I couldn't even see television.
My teddy bear and I were mad,
 My puppets and toys were sad.
As I looked through my darkened room,
 All I could see were witches on brooms.
I couldn't make out who they all were,
 but one was my mother of that I was sure.

Wouldn't it be wonderful if, whenever we were filled with anxiety because other people didn't live up to our expectations, all we had to do to relieve that anxiety was to pen our thoughts and feelings! This fifth-grade child learned to do this, as have many of our greatest persons.

Again, her anxieties after having a "rub in" with the teacher were expressed by these passages (repeated from Chapter VI).

my true thoughts

I feel like I want to say everything I think. It may not be a nice thing to do but the things I want to say aren't nice either. I am not aloud to cuss so I don't think I will, so how on Earth can I say the things I feel. I am about to burst and I feel like I am on fire. I am tense and my nerves are on edge. I am mad, I guess that's the best way to exspress my feelings. As I look around I see that no one is happy but 3 people but still I feel no better. Maybe I'll cool down by the end of the day but I seriously dought it. My eyes seem to be burning and tired. My cold seems to be getting worse and I find myself writing faster. I think I better forget what has happen today but it will be *hard*, but I am going to try *hard*!

The End

These passages were written very quietly, and were tucked away in her notebook. Perhaps no one would ever have seen them had she not been able to look back on those days and chuckle to herself about the problems that she faced.

Another aspect of Debbie's writing pattern indicated much eagerness to explore styles that other "better-known" writers had used. After the class had used the technique of bathos (described in Chapter IV) in some short pieces of description, Debbie wanted to apply the surprise ending to a larger story. The short stories of Poe and O. Henry were recommended for her reading. After she had read several of O. Henry's short stories and Poe's "The Pit and the Pendulum," she proceeded to write the following stories of her own, adapting a surprise-ending technique to the next four or five efforts. Here is "Blood Red."

Blood Red

It was dark in the area (stomp, stomp). A man was on his way home. It was quite dark and through the clouds of fog he made his way down the dark and quiet street. Through the fog he saw the address 1281 Longden and he knew he was home. He walked around the side of the house to the back door. Putting his key into the lock, he opened the door. It was quiet, even quieter than it was outside. He made his way to the lamp, he turned it on. He walked into the den where he slipped on something on the floor. It was wet and awfully gooey. He lit a soft light and he saw that the gooey substance was red Blood Red!! He grew tense and frightened and he knew that his wife and son had gone to a carnival. Had something happen to either of them? Neverously he went to his room. His heart was beating rapidly and he knew he was scared. He got a pain in his head that was unbearable. He felt his legs getting weak, then he slowly made his way to the telephone and all he had time to say was the first part of his address and that he needed help. He fell to the floor. The police and an amblance rushed to his home. He was taken to the hospital. When he awoke he was startled at first, for his wife was standing by the bed. He recalled what he had seen but found he could not talk. Apparently he had suffered a heart attack. He was watching her. After a minute she said you know when we came home from the carnival, I had so much to do and Junior didn't help matters much, he tried to make a catsup sandwich and spilled it all over the place.

The End

Such a simple plot! And such interesting insights to human behavior. Debbie's first attempt at the surprise-ending story was indeed a success. Her next three attempts follow in the order of completion. Notice the development of style and more complex themes as it is "taking place."

The Package*

London England—1776—December 2

It was a typical English day. It was cold, damp and foggy. It was the kind of a day when everything is quiet, very quiet. In the town square you could hear Big Ben's chimes echoing through the town. I had the feeling that I had to break the monotony and silence. How? As I stared out of my window I saw a figure in the foggy street. The figure was moving slowly, very slowly. It was the figure of an old person. The old man bothered me for some reason, so because there was nothing else to do, I decided to follow him. He was wearing old and ragged clothing. And what I could see of him told me that he had not had a shave in a long time. It seemed that the more I followed him the more he worried me. Finally he stopped in front of a very old building. I was not close enough to see what it was, but as I got closer I saw it was an old mortuary. I was throughally startled. I stood outside the frosted windows, awating the old man. Several minutes later the old man returned to the foggy street with a package. Now I felt I had to know what was in the package. I noticed that the old man's walk was getting faster so I started once more to follow him. This time he walked along the river Thames until he came to the bridge. It was usually foggy and damp near the water. The egerness to know what was in the package was overcoming me. The water seemed to roar very loudly. I just had to know. I stopped suddenly for the old man had stopped under the bridge. I could not see what he was doing for the fog. The fog started to lift. I saw the old man heading for the street. I was overcome with rage. I decided to walk faster. The faster I walked the faster the old man walked. Finally I was practicaly running. I caught up with him and I burst out, What was in it, what? The old man said What was in what? What are you talking about? In the package oh (ho ho). It was just a bunch of trash from the mortuary, you see I am a trash man and I always empty trash under the bridge.   **The End**

---

* Edited by the student.

Withering Heights

"It was fall, and in the mist of all the fallen leaves, there it was Withering Heights. No one had lived there for 25 years, but it still held momories in every cobweb. Through the years it had become a home for rodents, spiders, and bats. To my knowledge know one was living there at the present, so I thought that some day I might bring myself to explore it."

"When I was a kid, I remember going down to the creek, I would just sit there looking at the beautiful white pillared house."

"It was a early October morning when I decided to explore the house at Withering Heights. The only things I took with me were my knife; and a candle. The knife was to protect me from rats, and the candle was to find my way to a window to open the shade. Oh yes, I also took my lunch box full of sandwiches."

"I walked down to the creek, stopped and stared at the house and then went on across the creek. As I made my way throught the weeds, I looked ahead and only a few yards away there it stood, The once beautiful house at Withering Heights. The stone on the house had turned gray with dirt, and the gutters had been torn down by the wind. I moved forward and a rat darted across my feet, as if to tell me not to come any farther. But not paying much attention to it, I moved on. All kinds of thoughts were running through my head, but I did not let them bother me one bit. I walked up the cobblestone walk and there I was at the front door. I knocked, and when no one answered I went on in. Inside it was dark and the light from the open door showed the dirt and dust. There were a few old boxes and chairs and in the far corner was a wooden box that I thought was a trunk so I walked toward it, I looked at it for a minute, and then I started to lift the lid, the henges squeeked and then I saw it, I had never seen such a horrorable thing in all my life, It's teeth looked like the teeth of a Animal, his face looked powdery and white, and blood was dripping form his teeth, It was awful It didn't even look human. I jumped as a rat ran under my coat, after seeing the vampire I was awfully afraid, Bats were sleeping sound on the mantle. I ran to the door but it was locked. I turned around and there it was standing behind me (the vampire). The bats that were once a sleep on the mantle were on the vampire's shoulder. I ran up the stairs, but the vampire followed me. His eyes turned red and I felt myself growing tense. I was frightened. Running in fear I tore down the window shade. The sun shone in and the vampire hid his face and ran back to his casket growning. When my senses came back I realized what I had done, The light from the sun would destroy the vampire unless he was asleep. As I made my way down the stairs, through the dust I saw a painting on the wall. It was a young and handsome man, I glanced over at the vampire lying in the casket, there was a very large resemblance, not considering the teeth and paleness. When I reached the bottom of the steps, I walked toward the painting. There was a name at the bottom of the frame it read Sir John linton. I wrote the name down and walked toward the door, it opened, It was no longer locked. When I got home I got my departed mothers little book. I looked and looked and then finally there it was Sir John Linton. I was right the picture on the wall was sir John Linton and so was the vampire. I felt a chill go up my spine, I had a hard day. I blew out the candles and went to bed."

"In the middle of the night I was awakened by a cool breeze on my neck, I opened my eyes and I jumped just in time to keep my blood from getting drawn from my neck. I jumped from bed, I remembered what my father told me about vampires, and that two metal bars in the shape of a cross would kill them. I grabbed two bars and quickly formed a cross screeming: The vampire fell to the floor. It was awful, The vampire started slowly desinagrating, his arm, leg, and hands started turning to dust. I had destroyed a vampire. I lit all the candles, and when I got back, there was nothing left but a mound of dust. I took his ring to remember this night, not that I really want to.

The End

The Trial

SCENE I

Judge: "Are there anymore questions, Hamilton?"
Ham: "No your honor, thats all for now."
Judge: "Gentlemen and ladies, the day is late, the court is adjurned until tomorrow, when we will resume the case of Mr. Black versus Clark Johnson."

SCENE II (behind curtain have setting of room.)

Narrator:: "I would like to fill you in on what has happen so far. A picture worth $15,000 has been stolen from Edmund Black and his wife. They live at 1600 W. Ladden Rd. The picture is about 36" x 37", it is an abstract painting of a Peaso Bird. There are only 4 people who could have possibly taken it. 1. The Butler James, he is a tall dark-haired man, about 49 years old. He has been working for the Black family for over 4 years, and his only motive would be money, and he isn't the real rich. type. 2. The maid Anna has been working for the Blacks' for over 15 years, as a matter of fact she has been working for the Blacks' every since she was 18 years old." (open curtain, show Anna and James tidying up den.) "There could be no reason why she would want to take anything from the Black's' who have given her so much. And then theres old Aunt Bertha. She collects paintings herself, I surpose that would be her only motive. If it had been murder she would have the biggest motive, but robbery there is only a possibility. And last but not least there is the milkman, Clark Johnson who is the accused victim. He is friendly like most milkmen and has no enemies with the acception of Aunt Bertha. The reason he is the victim is because he is the only one with the acception of the Blacks' who has a key to the Blacks back door. Here we are in Hamilton's office where he and his secretary are dicussing the evidence."

SCENE III

Secretary: "Why would Mr. Johnson want to take the painting?
Hamilton: Well, why would you want a $15,000 painting?" "I would say for money."

Secretary: "Something is bothering me. Why would anyone give the milkman the key to their door? "Why couldn't he put the milk outside the door?"

Hamilton: "Well from what I see the Blacks' are very trusting people."

Secretary: "If its' true that the picture was taken between 1:00 a.m. and 4:00 a.m. then Mr. Johnson couldn't have taken it, because the president of the milk company he works for said he got there at that time and didn't leave until 4:10 a.m."

Hamilton: "May I refresh your memory?" "Mr. Johnson didn't report to work until 1:50 a.m. and the president said he didn't know where he was up till that time."

Secretary: "What about the butler? he could have taken is easily."

Hamilton: Anythings' possible Miss Gable."

Secretary: "I am trying to be serios Mr. Hamilton!"

Hamilton: "I am sorry, continue."

Secretary: "Well Mrs. McKinley . . .

Hamilton: (interupting) "Mrs. McKinley?—do you mean Bertha McKinley? the stubborn one?

Secretary: "Yes, Mrs. Blacks' Aunt Bertha, Well anyway she said the butler envied Mr. Black and didn't care for Mrs. Black, yet he needed money so he took the job."

Hamilton: "What do you think of Aunt Bertha?"

Secretary: "She isn't the friendly type thats for sure, I know I wouldn't like to have her for a aunt."

Hamilton: "As far as I found out she hasn't done anything before, but she seems jealous."

Secretary: "Well theres a first time for everything."

Hamilton: "Well theres only one person who could have done it and thats the maid." "But she is so nice and thankful for what she has, I really don't think she would take anything from the Blacks'."

Secretary: "Yes I like her a lot and I hope she had nothing to do with this robbery."

Hamilton: "Well courts tomorrow and I sure hope we get to the bottom of this."

SCENE IV—Courtroom (open curtain)

Narrator: "Here we are in the courtroom where we shall continue the case of the Black's versus Clark Johnson."

Judge: "Court will now come to order." "Mrs. Black would you please take the stand?" "Remember you are still under oath." "Mr. Hamilton."

Mrs. Black: "Yes your honor."

Hamilton: "What happen on the night of the 21st of May at approsmently 2:30 a.m.?"

Mrs. Black: "Well I was in bed and I heard a racket in the study and. . . . ."

Hamilton (interupting) "Mrs. Black how could you tell the noise was coming from the study?"

Mrs. Black: "Well the study is right over my room."

Hamilton: "Well continue."

Mrs. Black: "As I said, I was in bed when I heard a racket in the study." "Mr. Black wasn't home so I called for James my butler, he slept on the 3rd floor so I guess he didn't hear me." "I rang the bell, and about 2 minutes later Anna came with a flashlight." "Then we went to call the police, and when they got here who ever it was had gone."

Hamilton: "Are you quite sure that whoever did it had gone?"

Mrs. Black: "Well the police searched the house from top to botto, what do you mean?"

Hamilton: "Isn't it true that one of your own servants could have done it much easier than the defendent Mr. Johnson?"

Mrs. Black: "Yes, I surpose so, but. . . ."

Hamilton: "That will be all your Honor."

Judge: "You may cross examine the witness Mr. Carter."

Carter: "I have no further questions your Honor."

Judge: "You may step down Mrs. Black."

Carter: "May I call the defendent Mr. Johnson to the stand?"

Judge: "The defendant will take the stand."

Court Clerk: "State your name."

Mr. Johnson: "Clark Johnson."

C.C.: "Raise your right hand, do you solemnly swear to tell the truth, the whole truth and nothing but the truth so help you God?"

Mr. Johnson: "I do."

C.C.: "Take the stand."

Carter: "Where were you on the night of May 21st from 1:00 a.m. to 4:00 a.m.?"

Mr. Johnson: "Well I was at work."

Carter: "Exactly what time did you get to work?"

Mr. Johnson: "Well it was about 1:45 a.m."

Carter: (loudly) "Then you had 45 min. to go to the Blacks' home, take the painting and hide it then go to work is that right?"

Hamilton: (loudly) "Objection your honor, Mr. Carter is incinicating and he has nothing to base it on."

Judge: "Objection substained, Mr. Carter please restate your question?"

Carter: "I will, where were you from 1:00 a.m. till 1:45 a.m., on the night of the robbery?"

Mr. Johnson: "I was playing bridge with 3 friends of mine."

Carter: "Are these friends of yours here in court today?"

Mr. Johnson: "Two of them are, yes."

Carter: "Would you mind pointing them out?"

Mr. Johnson: "If it will help." "There they are sitting in the 2nd row on the left hand side." (point to men.)

Carter: "I have no further questions your honor."

Judge: "You may cross-examine the defendant Mr. Hamilton."

Hamilton: "I have no further questions your honor, but I would like to ask the man just described to please take the stand."

Judge: "Will Mr. Higgins, I think thats your name, please take the stand."

Hamilton: "Thank you your honor."

Court C.: "State your name."

Mr. Higgins: "Clarence Higgins."

Court C.: "Raise your right hand, do you solemnly swear to tell the truth, the whole truth and nothing but the truth, so help you God?"

Mr. Higgins: "I do."

Court C.: "Take the stand."

Ham.: "Do you testify that you were with Mr. Johnson the night of the robbery from 1:00 a.m. up till 1.45 a.m.?"

Mr. Higgins: "Yes I was with him, we were playing cards with a couple of fellas, as a matter of fact, I picked him up at 12:35 a.m., I remember looking at my watch."

Ham.: "Where did you play bridge at?"

Mr. Hig.: "We were at the home of the man I was sitting with." "He lives at 15 S. 8th st. "

Ham.: "What time did Mr. Johnson leave?"

Mr. Hig.: "He left with me it was about 1:20 a.m."

Ham.: "Where did you take Mr. Johnson?"

Mr. Hig.: "He said he could stand sme fresh air so I let him out of the car about 3 blocks from the milk company."

Ham.: "That will be all your honor."

Judge: "You may cross-examine the witness Mr. Carter."

Carter: "Thank you your honor, Mr. Higgins, had the defendent been drinking at all?"

Mr. Hig.: "Well you know how these bridge parties are."

Carter: "Surpose you tell *me* how they are."

Mr. Hig.: "Well just a little drink here and there."

Carter: (discussed) "That will be all your honor."

Judge: "You may step down now Mr. Higgins."

Ham.: "I would like to call Mr. Black to the stand your honor."

Judge: "Take the stand Mr. Black."

C. Clerk: "State your name."

Mr. Black: "Edmund Black."

C. Clerk: "Do you solemnly swear to tell the truth, the whole truth, and nothing but the truth, so help you God?"

Mr. Black: "I do."

C. Clerk: "Take the stand."

Ham.: "Mr. Black what time did you leave home on the night of May 21st?"

Mr. Black: "It was about 11:30 p.m."

Ham.: "Where did you go?"

Mr. Black: "I went to a party."

Ham.: "Why didn't your wife go also?"

Mr. Black: "She wasn't invited, it was a men's party, and what on Earth does this have to do with the robbery?"

Ham.: "It might have a lot to do with this particular robbery, what time did you get home?"

Mr. Black: "It was about 4;45 a.m."

Ham.: "Then you were gone all the time the robbery was surposed to have taken place?"

Mr. Black: "Yes I was."

Ham: "Was the painting insured?"

Mr. Black: "Yes it was but I still want it back?"

Ham: "Your honor if it please the court I would like a ten minute recess."

Judge: "That is a good idea and I think it is a good time to call a recess, court is adjurned until 2:30 p.m." (hit hammer on desk.)

Narr.: "Mr. Hamilton the attorney has had someone searching the Blacks' house."

Ham.: "He should be back in a while."

Secretary: "Yes, and I hope he hurries."

Narr.: "Ten minutes later, back in court." (open curtain)

Judge: "Order in the court."

C. Guard: (bust into courtroom.) "Your honor, this man insist on seeing Mr. Hamilton." (holding man by sleeve.)

Man: "I found it Mr. Hamilton, I did just as you said, I searched the Black's house and found it in Mr. Black's room, hidden."

Judge: "Order, order, please." "Now Mr. Hamilton would you give an explanation?"

Ham: "You see your honor, Mr. Black seemed so quick to accuse Mr. Johnson when he said he wasn't there when it happened and even though it was insured." "The way I see it is Mr. Black could collect the insurance and still have the painting."

Judge: "How do you explain the noise Mrs. Black heard."

Ham: "Evidently it was Mr. Black."

Judge: "Take him out." (Two court guards take him out.)

Narr. "And so Mr. Black got his."

The End

Two other efforts by Debbie are included here because they indicate the pattern variety with which some children (not all, by any means) can explore.

The Old Windmill*

In Holland there was a windmill which hadn't been used for over one hundred years. The people of Holland said it was a house for mice. This mill was just outside Amsterdam.

My story starts on a countryside six miles out of Amsterdam and one mile away from the mill. A little boy named Hans was sailing his boat in a canal near his home when it started to rain. He started home. On his way he saw the old mill. Walking toward it he slowly opened the door. It was very dark, he lit a match he found in his pocket. On the floor he saw a candle. Picking it up he lit it and blew out the match. A strong wind came and then blew the door shut. Hans ran to see if the door had locked and it had. Walking away from the door he saw a stairway. He started up. The steps screeched. When Hans got to the top he saw a window. Wiping it off he looked out. He saw that the river had increased considerably in size. Hans yawned, he dropped his sailboat and flopped down in a corner and fell fast asleep.

Quite a while later, he heard a roaring sound which awoke him. He stood up and looked out the window. The dike had broken! Water was everywhere and the canal where Hans had sailed his boat was now a roaring river. The mill was full of water. It was up to the fifth stair and had four stairs to go. Hans swam to the hatch which started the mill. It was rusty and a small boy like Hans could not possibly move it. Suddenly he got an idea. Climbing the steps, he looked out the window. He reached his hand out as far as he could and finally he grabbed the fan of the mill. The motor started and all the water was going through the mill and pumping the land dry.

About that time in Amsterdam, patrol boats were going out to look for Hans whose mother was getting very worried. After

* Edited by the student.

Hans got tired of turning the fan of the mill he let go and the wind took over. All of a sudden, Hans heard sirens. He looked out of the window and he was overjoyed when he saw the patrol boats. He took out his handkerchief and flagged the patrolman down. One patrolman saw Hans and turned his boat toward the mill. The patrolman called to Hans, "Are you all right?"

Hans answered, "Yes." He started down the steps.

The patrolman said, "Did you start this old rusted thing all by yourself?"

Hans replied, "Yes."

On the way back to Amsterdam the patrolman told Hans that he had saved Amsterdam from a terrible disaster, that could have killed many people. Hans felt proud.

If you ever go to Holland look for the countryside six miles out of Amsterdam and one mile away from the mill.

Herman the Ant.*

1. *The Plot*

My story takes place in Black Willow. You start from Austin Texas and go north then south then east then west, and you follow the river to its end and there it is an anthill town. There are anthills of all sizes. Since it is a western town there are salons, hotels, and dry good stores. There are also ranches and cafe's. Of course they are all made of sand and dirt, and they are made by the hard labor of the ants that live there. First we'll meet the hard working bulls eye shooting marshel Wyatt Slurp. And then theres sissor happy, whiskey drinken Doc Holly. Oh, and we mustn't forget puppy the salon gal. The leader of the biggest gang in black willow is Trigger Sagholster, he's a rooten tooten cowboy, If I've ever seen one. Well I am Herman and I am going to tell you a story about our town. It happen about 12 years ago, Matt Dill-pickle and his sons blacky and Jacky were on their way into town when they saw an ant lying in the road. They recogized him as

---

* Edited by the student.

Sherlock Bones. Sherlock Bones was a rancher who had been living in black willow. Matt Dillpickle replied to his sons, by cracky It's old Bones. After they buried him under 1" of dirt, which was quite a lot they went on toward town. Sherlock Bones was a good friend of Matt and his sons so he wanted revenge. When he got to town he went to marshel Slurp protesting that he find the murderer. He said, I found my pal Sherlock Bones lying in the road full of buckshot, and I am not going to forget it until the ant that murdered him is hanging from the thread on my mouses saddle. He left full of rage. He headed for the Short Branch salon. As he approached the short Branch he heard, Yes siree I shot him down dead that old Bones will never flurt with my susabell again. Then he heard someone say come on and have some more whiskey Wild Bill Hichead. This was all an ant could stand, he went tearing into the short Branch like lightning striking a tree. He said, all right which one of you is wild Bill Hichead. A man 6'6" stood up and said, I am the ant your looking for if your looking for wild Bill J. Hichead. Matt Dillpickle said well er al I mean ther must be some kind of mistake I am so sorry. Shivering Matt left the Short Branch. But like any stupid coward he was still determined to get Revenge.

2. Revenge

Matt thought If I shot him in the back I would become a cruel man, and If I poisoned him It wouldn't be very nice. I have to find some ant like way. The next day Matt with the help of his sons and Trigger sagholster, thought of the perfect way. Here were his plans. He would drop a gold map in front of W. Bill's hotel room. The map would lead him into Indian ant territory and naturally the Indians would skin him alive. It worked!!

The End

Thom

The second group of selections is most interesting. Written by Thom and only three in number, they present a gamut of forces at work. When asked, for instance, to write out the process of multiplication (a teacher check on his understanding level) he wrote the following. (See also Figures 5 and 6.)

Multiplication

$$43$$
$$\times 38$$

Eight times 3 is 24. Carry the 20 into the tens column over the 4 in 40. And write the four in 24 down in the ones answer column. Then Multiply 8 times 4, (really 8 times 40); which is 32 (320) and add the two that I carried. Now multiply 3 times 3, (30 times 3) which is 9 (90). Then multiply 3 times 4, (30 times 40) and that is 12 (1,200). Now add 0 and 4 which is 4. And 4 and 9 (40 and 90) which is 13 (130) and carry the ten. And add 2 and 3 and the 1 (200 and 300 and 100) that I carried in the last column adds up to 6 (600). And the thousand column only has one thousand in it so we don't have to add that. The total answer to this whole blasted problem is: 1,634
one thousand, six hundred, thirty four.

A real comedian plays the comic role even in arithmetic class! Tommy Turtle (as he was called by his mates) didn't think he was doing his best work when he wrote comedy. He felt he knew what the class liked, however; and many times he kept his "more serious" thoughts and ideas to himself. The following descriptive piece indicates the sensitivity of this sixth-grader—for a while, at least—and then, in a group-pleasing climax, he adds a final touch.

I am thinking of a day and place where nothing could go wrong, a slight breeze, the puffed clouds above a chrystal-blue lake; an inlet to the lake which has carved a path; with the clear water trickling over the rocks. This day is a lazy type day; the kind that you can just sit, without being bored. This place I'm talking about is spotted with tall fur and pine trees. The ground is covered with pine needles fallen years before, and it is about 1½ inches thick so it makes a nice soft padding. Now you and I are leaving this lovely place, going the trail which follows the inlet and passes little fir trees about 4 inches tall. We have just finally gotten back to the canoes, WHEN—

SUDDENLY—— A *turtle* came up to me, and said, TOMMY!! I HAVEN'T SEEN YOU AROUND THE OLD WATERS ANYMORE!!

Division In fractions

Thom Randall

$6\frac{1}{2} \div 3\frac{1}{4}$ I think . I Know how to do this. The first thing I'll do now is to change the 6 and 3 into fractions $6\frac{1}{2}$ is the same as $\frac{13}{2}$ and $3\frac{1}{4}$ is the same as $\frac{13}{4}$ so I will use them. Now the problem looks like this: (see figure #1)

Figure #1: $\frac{13}{2} \div \frac{13}{4}$

divisor upside down. Now I multiply! Now I will turn the (I still don't understand why.) (see figure #2 and 3.)

Figure 2: $\frac{13}{2} \div \frac{13}{4} \cancel{5}$ SO--- Figure 3: $\frac{13}{2} \cdot \frac{4}{13}$ Now here

I go mutiplying. 4 times 13 is 52; and 2 times 13 is 26. the answer is $\frac{52}{26}$ but it can be broken down to 2. And that is the total answer.

FIGURE 5

Tommy also had some talent as a ventriloquist. His sidekick was named Jerry Maloney, and for script Thom would write play after play of slapstick. Included here is "Jerry of the Apes." (Occasionally the plays written by Tommy were used in dramatic sessions with classmates sharing roles.)

ADDING FRACTIONS   T. Randall

$$25 \frac{5}{8} = \frac{5}{8}$$
$$+16 \frac{3}{4} = \frac{6}{8}$$
$$42 \frac{3}{8}$$

My Arithmetic problem <u>now</u> is twenty-five and five eighths add sixteen and three fourths. Now the first thing I should tackle is to make 4ths into 8ths. I make the three fourths into Eighths so I can work this problem accuratley and easily... Three-fourths is the same as six-eighths so that's what I change them into. NOW: This is what we have: $\frac{5}{8} = \frac{5}{8}$ NEXT: We add $\frac{6}{8}$ to $\frac{5}{8}$. That adds up to $\frac{11}{8}$. In $\left\lfloor +\frac{3}{4} = \frac{6}{8} \right\rfloor$ other words, 1 and $\frac{3}{8}$. Then we carry the 1 into the ones column. $+16 \frac{3}{4}$. Now we add 25 and 16; which is ..... Lets see! ------ 8 and 5 -------- 11 ----- carry the one----- 1, 1, and 2 ---- ---- let's see ---- 4 ------- 4 1! Oh Yes! The one I carried 42! Let's see. Hmmm. I forgot the $\frac{3}{8}$. How (Terrabul)! Let's add this up now! ----- 40 ---------- ---- oh yes! one two----------- and the $\frac{3}{8}$ --- --- --- --- --- ---

THE WOLD'S FASTEST, CALCULATING ELECTRONIC BRAIN <u>SAYS</u> ----- — — — ----- The answer to this problem is 42 and $\frac{3}{8}$.

What is a <u>WOLD</u>?

FIGURE 6

JERRY OF THE APES

Announcer: Our story starts as a safari is wandering through Africal.

(curtains open)
(JUNGLE SCENE)

Guide: Bwana! we is all goofed up—I don't know where we is!

Captain: We can't stop now! If we go back, the white Rama will kill us for swiping his bottle!

Jean: EKK! Look! A lion!

Jerry (cry from off stage): Ah-ee-ah-ee-ah! ee-ah-ee-ah!

Captain: What's that?

Guide: That's Jerry of the apes! He'll save us!

Jerry: (coming in on vine—I guess!): What you want?

Jean: Jerry! Save us! Save us from the lion!

Jerry: Lion! LION! LION?? Hey! Nobody told me ther'd be a *lion* in this play! Where's that producer!

Producer: What do you want?

Jerry: Do I have to fight that lion?

Producer: Sure!

Jerry: Mr. Pease! MR. PEASE!

Mr. Pease (coming on stage): Yeah?

Jerry: Can you knda—quit a play?

Mr. Pease: No quitting plays!

Jerry: Wah! I'm too young to die!

Guide: Do you actually think that we would use a real lion? That's Teddy!

Jerry: It don't look like Teddy!

Guide: Dope! He has a costume on! Look! Teddy! Teddy!

Teddy (Running on stage): You want me?

Guide: T-T-T-Teddy! If your here, who's the lion?

Lion: ROAR!!!!

(EVERYONE RUNS OFFSTAGE)
(Curtains close)

Announcer: There will be a slight intermission, folks!

Lion (Peeking through curtains): Why Not?

Announcer: Getting on with the story, the safari went on until they found a house. They went into it, and the rest you'll see now!

(Curtains open)

(Haunted house scene)

Jene: (Ulp!) I-I-I-I w-wonder w-w-who lives h-h-here.

Captain: You tell me!

Jene: Willy-Willy! What are you doing over by that box?

Guide: I'm—well, I thought I saw it move!

Captain: Willy-Willy, when we go back to the states, remind me to have your eyes checked!

WHILE SAFARI GOES ON THROUGH THE ROOM, A MUMMY STEPS OUT OF THE MUMMY CASE. THE MUMMY WALKS OVER AND KIDNAPS WILLY-WILLY! THEN PUTS WILLY-WILLY IN THE MUMMY CASE, AND PUT'S A "DO NOT DISTURB" SIGN ON IT.

Jene: Where's Willy-Willy?

Captain: I don't kn—Ahhh (TURN'S AROUND AND REVEALS ARROW IN STOMACH).

Jene: EEEEK!!!!

Jerry (from off-stage): AH-EE-AH-EE-AH! EE-AH-EE-AH!

Jene: Is that you, Jerry?

Jerry: (Flying in on vine) Me Jerry, You Jene! What you want?

Jene: Get me out of here!

Jerry: Uh—How?

Jene: What do you mean? You got in here, didn't you?

Jerry: Yeah, but I don't know the way out! (Jerry, going over to the door) Maybe this is the way out!

Jerry opens door and reveals Willy-Willy hanging from nuce)—

Jene: EEEK! AHH! EEEK! A MOUSE!!!

Jerry: Me get you out of here! AH-EE-AH-EE-AH-EE-AH-EE-AH!!!

Guy from upstairs: LOOK, BUDDY——

Jerry: Why are you?

Guy from upstairs: I'M DAH GUY FRUM UPSTAIRS!!!!

Jerry: Sorry, I didn't know you were sleepin'!

Guy from upstairs: I was'nt! I was trappin' bed bugs! Look buddy, if I hear any more racket down here, you is gonna answer ta' me!!!!!

Jerry: Oh, don't worry about Me makin' racket! I do'nt even play *TENNIS* ! ! ! ! ! HA!HA!HA!HA!HA!—

Guy from upstairs (Hitting Jerry in the jaw): OW! You broke my wittle hand! You broke my wittle hand! (Then pointing at Jerry's head) Now dat's whut I call a *NUMB-SKULL*! ! ! ! !

    (Guy from upstairs walks away)

Jerry: Well, how are we gonna get outa here?

Jene: Try calling the butler!

Jerry: O.K ! BUTLER! BUTLER!

Laugh from off-stage: UM-WAH- AH-AH-AH-Ah! ! !

Jene: Who did that?

Jerry: The butler did it! ! !

    (Crash) (Bang! BANG!) (Boom)

Jene: Who did that?

Jerry: The butler did it! He has tummy-rumbles!"

Jene: It couldn't be! WILL SOMBODY TELL ME WHO DID THAT?

Beatnic: Maybe it was like a burglar!

Jean: Then what should we do?

Beatnic: Buzz a fuzz!

Jene: Where's a phone?

Beatnic: Give me a Washington!

Jene (taking out dollar and giving it to him): Here!

Beatnic: I'm with you!

Jean (excitedly): Come on! Where's the phone?

Beatnic: Like, what's the caper? Fill me in!

Jene: Well, we're trapped in here!

Beatnic: Like, you gotta use——

Midnight.

chapte**1**. interducing Midnight.

Mu! mu! my name is Midnight
I'm a cat-black, now frist
of all, here is my history!
I used to work for a wicht
but after two years of
that I was fried on
pretence unknown to me.
After that I got a job,
in a bucher shop but
didnt stay there long
because I was the one
they were going to buch-
er. so you see, well-a-you
know. what I mean.
And ontop of all that
I was haveing kittens
every six moths.
So by now I figured
that life was just one.
damm buch of kittens

FIGURE 7

after other with
troble inbetween! well
any way I'm going to tell
you my most exsiteing
story so here we
go

FIGURE 8

Chris

The third group demonstrating writing style and technique was written by Chris. Probably the most prolific elementary school "writer" the author has ever had opportunity to work with, Chris was once asked if he ever thought he would like to write as a professional. He replied, "Oh, I'll do all my writing in my spare time!"

His cat, named Midnight, was a very special pet, and often served as a theme for his written explorations. Some passages from his "Midnight" stories follow. (See also Figures 7 and 8.)

Midnight

Chapte 1.   interducing Midnight.

Mu! Mu! my name is Midnight I'm a cat—black, now frist of all, here is my history! I used to work for a wicht but after two years of that I was fried on pretence unknown to me. After that I got a job in a bucher shop but did'nt stay there long because I was the one they were going to bucher. So you see, well—a—you know what I mean. And ontop of all that I was haveing kittens every six moths. So by now I figured that life was just one damm buch of kittens after other with troble in between!

His story continued, and later in another of his series, he wrote about "Halloween in Heaven," by Midnight.

Chapter 1 going!

I was sitting on cloud no. 999,999 when an angle dispacther flew down and handed me a letter, "big boy (God) says your premoted to cloud 1,000,000 and flew off. I opened the letter, it read:

Dear Middnight
I am glad to inform you that your are
transferred to cloud 1,000,000
Your boss!
God

YHOO!

You see I always wanted to go to 1,000,000 because 999,999 was an all girls cloud, 1,000,000 was mostly— WOW! WOW! boys.

Well, at 10:am central cloud time I got on the camuter bus. At 12 I got off on cloud 1,000,000.

chapter 2 there!

I walked around for abit, then I saw my earth romance. "ALLEY"! I yelled. "MIDDNIGHT", he exclaimed."Middnight", he said, "I want you to meet a frind of mine, Tabby, this is Middnight." "Hi Tab."
"Hi Mid."
The next night was Holloween,"what's Holloween like up here?" I asked.
"I don't know I'v only been up here for three moths.
"Oh!"
"Yeah."
Then suddenly Brring! Brring! "Whats that?"
"The warning bell, something grave must of happened," answered Tabby.
"Come on we'd better get down the cloud house."
"Yeah, come on."

Three minutes later we were at the cloud house and the govener of cloud 1,000,000 was makeing a speech.

chapter 3 Geting ready!

"Dear friends and neigbors, to come right down to it I am asking
for vollnteers to save heaven from a fate incomparable to any
we've even seen or heard of, a foreign object come up from the
devil's Kingdom to destroy heaven. We do'nt know how heavily
it's armed, but! As I said befour, we do know that it's from the
devil's relm. I'm asking for vollenteers." Tabby raised his hand
"You crazy", I wispered!
"I like adventure."
"Aren't you going to extrems?"
"Nope!" so I raised my hand, you see I wanted to keep tabs on
Tabby and Alley wanted to keep tabs on me. (I consider my self
pretty.) So three hands were in the air. "All right", said the govener,"You and you and you"!, he said pointing to Tabby Ally and
I. "You leave tomorrow morning."
That night I paked the things I thought we might want, they were:
1. A jakeknife. 2. 2 cartons of beer. 3. A pistol for each of us. 4. 50
feet of rope. 5. A devil costume for each of us. 6. Glasses for the
beer. (we were tidy cats) 7. A magic food maker. (But we could'nt
work it) 8. A radio to listen to the football games. and last of all
boxing gloves incase we got mad at each other.

And so on. Chris wrote another of the same series, entitled "Midnight and the Moose That Knew a Goose Who Was a Relative of
a Sorcerers Zoose!" And that he could write description is evident
in the following.

The long gray arms of the mist reached out over the ground. The
moon was half covered by clouds as one lone star shone shimering
in the south. The erie sound of a far off siren reached my ears as
the sky began to clear. In the still air there was a movement, an ,
unearthly movement, as if the air itself were living, thinking. The
shadows of the night creatures of the past, the present, and perhaps the future flowed throug my mind as a never ending piture
as I made my way up the narrow mountain trail. The sky was

clear up here and the stars shone brightly upon the mountain tops. And I felt alone in another world cut off from my homelad. And so high was I that I was in a world beyound the world with the whole of nature spread before me. And above me there was beuty, and below there was beuty. And streacted out along the horizon the never ending adventure of life. I felt the pride of discovery, for I was the first to see it. I was on the summit of Mt. Everest, the first, the first of all mankind.

As a fifth-grader, Chris wrote a book entitled "A Long Way From Here to There." When he was preparing to begin his story, he made an outline of experiences and adventures to be included in the novel about space travel. His outline ended: "I think I'll end it [the story] with a poem by Robert Frost: 'Two roads converged in the woods, and I took the one less traveled—thereby making all the difference.'"

Pictures of this book (published by the family, for the family and friends) appear in Figures 9–12. Pictures of the original manuscript (167 pages long in Chris's own handwriting) show the use of stress words, the use of diagrams and pictures to help the reader prepare for the chapters to come, and the variety of paper types used in the writing. It is the idea that really counts in the original manuscript. If necessary (and meaningful), editing can always follow later.

In his writing efforts Chris had advanced to a value stage at which he seldom needed the group evaluation and encouragement that are so important in peer motivation and reinforcement. As a result, he would select only some of the highlights of his efforts for sharing with the group.

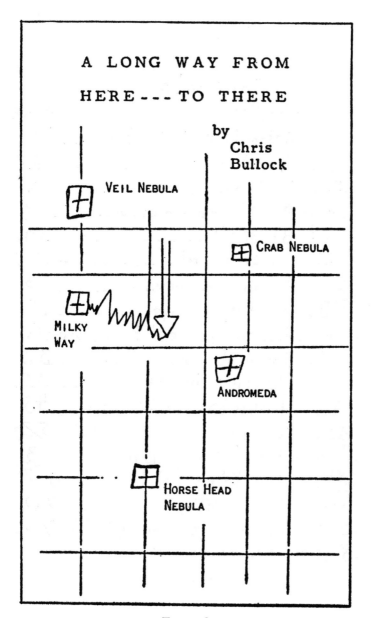

Figure 9

Contents

chapter page

I. Astroids and disaster........ 1.

II. Operation rescue.............. 6.

III. Missing men............. 11.

IV. A ship and a crew...... 15.

V. Blast of.................. 19.

VI. Jupiter bound................ 22.

VII. A long jorney.............. 25.

VIII. Saturens rings.............. 29.

IX Missing fuel and found papers. 34.

X. Beyound soturen......... 37.

XI Muitiny in space..... 38.

XII Missiels! look out!.... 43.

XIII Eescape and fighT.... 52.

XIV The deception....... 63.

XV The imposiable!..... 67.

XVI Thought............. 70.

XVII Horro from pluto.. 75.

XVIII. Descovry

FIGURE 10

May
1969

Chapter 21.

A citiy for science.

Jim walked over to the other opening there was dim glow inside, Jim know had taken of his

FIGURE 11

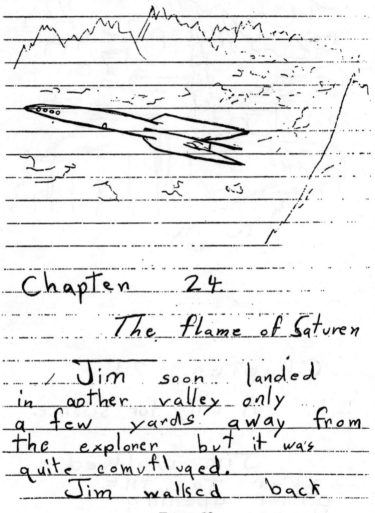

Chapter 24

The flame of Saturen

✓ Jim soon landed
in aother valley only
a few yards away from
the exploner but it was
quite comufluged.
Jim wallsed back

FIGURE 12

Eric

Not all patterns, of course, are as highly developed as the three mentioned thus far. Consider the problem faced by Eric.

When a child suddenly finds himself in a situation where writing is fun, and where writing is a natural way of learning and expressing himself, that child can have several reactions. If he himself has had some experience at writing, then the new situation will likely be rewarding and non-threatening. If, however, he comes into the situation with no background in writing at all, much frustration will likely exist. "Frustration" is the correct term to describe Eric's feelings.

Eric entered the group as a sixth-grader, and without previous writing experiences. He wanted to write, and he tried hard to write something he could be satisfied with. But (as must often be asked) where was Eric setting his standards? Were they realistic for a beginner? Likely not, since the only contact that Eric had with written materials were contacts with polished manuscripts, books, things by professional writers. Like all children who do not get an early start at writing, Eric's standards were not realistic for his beginning abilities. Standards and abilities should be allowed to develop naturally, throughout the elementary program.

Eric understood that this possible cleavage (standard–ability) existed, and he attempted to prove to himself that he could write. Here are some of the writings he thought were acceptable; notice the ideas in his writings that sixth-graders might not usually be sensitive to.

No. 1

warm misty rain falling gently to the ground
blinding fog makes birds flight helpless
soft winds blow rain briskly through trees
rain drops pitter patter against soft earth

No. 2

snow scurries every which way
darting foward towards earth
laying its crystal mass
on every object in sight

No. 3

Strong sun beams shine through green leafted trees,
Swiftly but unoticed a little breese swept past silently,
A few leaves or a twig might have fallen on the ground,
Even for a few seconds sun light hid between two clouds and
    then reapered,
One or two squrrels were gathering nuts for winter sulplies,
As sun hid in the west at night.

John

Often a child who finds it difficult to express himself verbally will be able to adapt quite capably to the art of written expression. John, our fifth contributor, was such a child, and in almost all that he wrote he exhibited the important attitudes and values by which he lived. Cleverly humorous, John's level of satire and comedy was often beyond comprehension of his classmates, even though they were often implied as characters in his writings.

John had difficulty in expressing his ideas verbally, but look what he could do when he wrote a report (see page 115; see also Figures 13 and 14).

FROM APE TO MAN
IN A MILLION YEARS

BY JOHN VOLKER

with extreme

gratitude to

THOMSON RANDALL

FROM APE TO MAN IN A MILLION YEARS

TABLE OF CONTENTS

FROM APE TO MAN IN A

MILLION YEARS

BY JOHN VOLKER

DEDECATED TO:

WILLIAM THOMSON

RANDALL

FOR HIS SUPREME

ASSISTANCE THAT MADE

THIS BOOK POSSIBLE

★COPYRIGHT 1960 T&J PUBLISHING CO.

Figure 13

CHAPTER 1 THE EVOLUTION OF MAN

Before Darwin, Man reasoned with himself that he was the same in ancient times as he was then and always would be. But modern science disproved that fact. The two bettling theories are that of Darwinism and the Bible. The Bible says that Adam and Eve were the first humans on earth, but the theory of human evolution (Darwin; ape to man) says that man came from the anthropoids. Neither of these theorys have ever been disproven.

Human Evolution, as Darwin call it, is suposed to have started with an odd, ape-like creature, the Pithecanthropus Erectus, and gone up, gradually decreasing in hair and other ape-like charicteristics.

When we say the word "human" and the word "apes," many people take it for granted that apes are not human, in a sense, that they cannot think. It is my theory that apes and other animals can think, and it is not entirely instinct.

Did you ever stop to think what makes us go to sleep at nights, and wake up in the morning?* That's instinct. Did you ever stop to think when we touch something hot, and we pull our hands away, what made us do that? *Instinct!* An so apes are'nt much different from man, and, as modern science improves, we might even find out that animals really do think.

CHAPTER 2 THE "MISSING LINK"

For many years, as man was studying anthropology, he had what seemed like an unsolvable mystery. For when they tried to figure out what species of creature was in between ape and man, it was like a road to nowhere. Science was so bewildered that they just called it the missing link in the chain of human evolution. Some men actually combed the world for a live man who had been dead 500,000 to 1,000,000 years. In fact, the term "Missing Link" became so popular,

---

*I DON'T MEAN OUR MOTHERS.

that circuses and carnivals often featured men dressed up oddly in cages and called them that.

In 1891, Eugene Dubois, a French surgeon in the Dutch Colonial Army uncovered a fossilized thigh bone, three fossilized teeth, and a fossilized skull-cap. These five fragments of bone were one of the most important discoveries in modern anthropology. For these bones were of the Pithecanthropus Erectus, or ape man of Java, as he is more commonly termed.

The average Pithecanthropus Erectus was five foot six inches in heith. The name Erectus signafies that he walked erect, a position that no ape can assume. The Pithecanthropus Erectus has been called a number of names. A few of them are "Missing Link," Java Man, Java Ape-Man, Trwil Man, and just plain Pithecanthropus Erectus.

On a later date, a more complete pithecanthropus skull was found. Natives working for this party found it, and smashed it, and gave it to them piece to get more money.*

A relative of the Pithecanthropus Erectus is the Pithecanthropus Robustus who's habitat was usually around lower Africa.

Another primitive species of African men was the Rhodesian Man. In this name, as most all other names of primitive races, you can tell where he was from by the name, as Rhodesian Man was from Rhodesia.

CHAPTURE 3   PEKING MAN AND HEIDELBERG MAN
AND PILTDOWN MAN

Peking Man, (Sinanthropus), was discovered in 1929 by Davidson Black in Peking, China. Some scientists think that this sub-human species may be the forerunner of certain types of mongolians.

Heidleberg Man was discovered in Mauer, Germany. This place was close to Heidelberg, so the discoverers named it the Heidleberg Man. The heidelberg man is sometimes referred to as Homo Heidelbergensis.

The Heidelberg man is believed to be the oldest of the sub-men

-----

*Who say natives are'nt smart?

that once enhabited Western Europe, and the ancestor of a later species of human, the Neanderthal Man. The piltdown man was believed to have perished during the second glacial wave.

Piltdown Man, (Eoanthropus Dawsoni), was discovered in Sussex, England (close to Piltdown). He was discovered in 1911-1912 by Charles Dawson. The Piltdown Man is often refered to as dawn man. The petrified skeleton was found with a petrified wooden club that may have belonged to him.

CHAPTURE 4 NEANDERTHAL AND CRO-MAGNON MEN

Neanderthal Man was discovered in Heidelberg, Germany in 1865, and was believed to have lived 300,000 years ago. The reason he got his peculuar name, was because he was found near the Neander River. He has two names refering to his body structure. These names are Homo Sapians Sapians, and the other is Homo Neanderthalsis.

Cro-Magnon man was believed to live 14,000 years ago, so that will give you an idea of how short it takes for humans to change. The Cro-Magnon is believed to have been the most advanced of the primitive men. For he could make fire, he had bows and arrows, and even had dishes and bowls which were most advanced. The Cro-Magnon man, in fact, could speak just about the way we could, and probably better than some of us. There was'nt much difference between modern man and the Cor-Magnon man, except for certain small items. It's like certain cars who come out the same two years in a row, there are'nt many differences you can see on the surfaces, but, when you get right down to it, there are some minor differences. The Cro-Magnon man was so alike modern man, that we have named him Homo Sapians, the same name as modern science terms us.

So as you think about these primitive men, remember: They weren't much different than you. They had feelings and they thought and wondered the same as you. What they thought, we cannot say definitely. But from what we can guess, they thought about the world around them, the stars above them, the fear inside them: The fear of the unknown. Perhaps they wondered about lightning, and of its tremendous light that was like harnessed fire, thrashing in the rain; or perhaps they wondered about thunder, and it's loud noise that broke the silence of the rainy night; or perhaps they thought about fire; it's amazing abilities; and perhaps they wondered about the properties of fire. It wasn't a liquid. It wasn't a solid. It was like a weightless liquid that didn't feel like a liquid at all. What did they think about? What did they wonder about. Scientists are amazing people but they cannot read minds. They can assume to tell the physical properties of man, but never; I repeat—NEVER will they conquor the mental properties of man.

And to top that effort off, after he had finished writing the "From Ape to Man" report, he was asked if he could do a cartoon-type illustration of his personal interpretations concerning his subject. Not more than fifteen minutes later he submitted the cartoon strip in Figure 14.

John's humor was the most adult-like that the writer has ever witnessed in a child. Figure 15 is a Halloween cartoon, done about two weeks after Sputnik No. 1.

John's verse style is illustrated by the following.

No. 1

The Peas-O Bird was sitting on a rock,
Along came the Peasett bird, and boy did they talk!
"C'mon'n have some coffee—direct from Case-Blanke!
Said Peasett "I'll play a pranke, 'n' drop a hankie in his sank-e!
"HA-HA! I beecha' to it! The Peas-o said with ease,
"You Big Ole Rottin' apple! I'm go' tell Mr. Pease!
"C'mon, Ferget it Baby! Werr steppin' out tonight!
"Now Yer talkin' Honey!" "It's sure a loosin' fight!"

No. 2

In a dark and muddy terrain,
Some feathers sit out in the rain,
In the wet and dreary night,
As the rain comes down with great might.

And the lightning flashes so bright—
I wonder, is that bird insane?
Ther bird gets up with a terrible fight.
and vanishes into the mist of the night.
Then he comes back with a bottle of beer,
And emties the whole bottle into his ear.

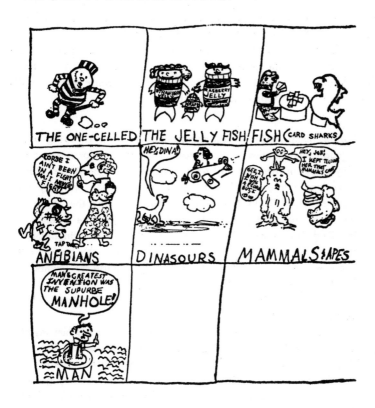

"From Ape To Man"

FIGURE 14

And then he lay down like the mud was a bed
If you ask me I think he is touched in the head.
This went on for many a day,
Until the men in the white suits came and carried him away.

More tensions, perhaps, were released in the following two selections. John's first, "Definition of Parents," indicates the sensitivity with which children view their own behavior as well as the behavior of adults. The second, of which only portions are included, gives indications of the tremendous variety of fairly sophisticated concepts which most children come by naturally but never have opportunities to express.

Parents jump at the littlest things! For instance: Throwing a ball through Mr. Jones'es window, trading my tricycle for a watch that Billy found in Mrs. Jonson's trash can, chopping down Mr. Masons prize apple tree, hitting Mrs. Walker's bull dog with my sling shot, squirting Dad's Boss with the hose, pushing the Teacher in the swimming pool, throwing Dad's cufflinks out the window, using Dad's rich uncle's ties for the tail on my kite, bringing home a cat-like animal with a white stripe going down his back. I don't know why they jumpped out the window, 'cause he smelled just like Mom's perfume.

The time they relly blew there top was the time, well, I'll tell you about it.

It was 3:00 and I went out to meet Dad and tell him my side of the story. Well, on the way I met Ronnie. It was her 3rd birthday and I had a present for her. I had saved up my allounce and bought her a genuine 25¢ deck of cards for our weekly game of strip poker. I gave her the present and she opened it up. "GEE!!! A genuine deck of cards." SMACK!!! Well, that was that!!! Any way, I met Franky and we went down to the football feild and took the ball. This man, I think he said his name was Robin—No! It was Bob White, caught us and we were held in the lockerroom. Franky had the ball and went up to Hoppalong Cassidy and he took the

Halloween in 1958

FIGURE 15

ball and write on it. Then he passed it along to the others, and they wrote on it. When we got home, Dad was just about to send us to reform school when I showed him the ball. SMACK! ! ! Two kisses in one day I can't stand! ! !

The End

Excerpts from "Chris, the Crater-Cleaner":

No. 1

There was a moonling named Chris. He cleaned craters. One day as Chris was cleaning his craters he noticed a strange craft heading towards him. It landed on his broom with a bristling noise.

Chris hollered, "Get this stupid machine off my crater-broom! These danged Russians and their high flying rockets!"

"Chris, Chris", said Paul Von Hoffman, the greatest scientist this side of the moon. "Are you all right?"

"Yeah, I guess so—but I'll have to get a new broom", said Chris. "Come on, Paul—let's go over to the next crater. I want you to meet a friend of mine."

Chris and Paul went over to the next crater where they saw another moonling with a goatee and a beret reciting poetry to himself.

"Be outta' getcha in a push-cart baby,
Better be ready by five 'till seven!
I got a date with another lady,
I gota' be home by eleven!
No, that's terrible! That's no good!
I'm gonna make a poem about food!
Not apples! Not peaches! Not plums or marsetti,
I'm gonna make one about SPEGETTI!
That beautiful, beautiful, delectable dish!
It's not like fruit or meat or fish!
It's—" just then Chris enterupted

No. 2

"That tea dunker never showed an interest in girls in his whole dad-burned, cotten-picken, booze bottleing, jug drinkin', moon-shine makin' life!"

"I don't mean that!"

"Thank's loads!"

"No, No! What I had in mind was maybe we could convince Tea-dunker to drink milk like Billy Goat Hammerhead!"

"Sure, Now all we have to do is to find a cow that gives 150 proof milk!

"Maybe you couldn't find a cow, but I could rig up a goat."

"That gives 150 milk? Why don't you give up, Billy!"

"No, No! I mean I could ask Theadore Issac Fignewtonhess the anylist to make milk taste like moon shine!"

"They said, it couldn't be done!"

"What couldn't be done, Tommy?"

"Booze from Moo's?"

"Oh, Thommy, your a nut!"

"They said it couldn't be done.

They said nobody could do it.

But booze

From moo's,

Is low in proof, with more milk to it!"

"Teadunker, you spoiled all are plans."

"Well, Kay spoiled my appetite. Man! She kisses like a 1920 ford with it's hood open!"

An urgency to express one's ideas in one's own way! We all have it. Certainly that urgency can be felt in the writings of those children so graciously contributing to these pages.

Many times a child's aggressive behavior can be released through written expression that is sensitive, affectionate, and humorous—and eagerly accepted by both children and teachers.

The examples of writing previously noted and commented upon are but indications of the following patterns:

1. Children can become very versatile in both style and type of writing.
2. Children can release much emotional tension through writing of various types and styles.
3. Children explore concepts, newer and older, and the ways in which these concepts are related to themselves personally, through written experience.

Accepting the child as he is (a complex of tensions and adjustment techniques), then providing for his further development, is the goal of all teachers. Many of the written expressions of children help us as teachers to know more about the tensions and adjustment techniques that are influencing the behavior of the individual child.

First Time Skating

by C. V.

I went skating Friday noon
I went falling awful soon!

I tried to make a figure eight,
But all I got was a broken skate.

I was pretty good at last
All my falls were in the past.

When you go skating,
                    take my advice,
Better go skating on cotton ice!

CHAPTER VIII

A CASE STUDY OF
ONE CHILD'S WRITINGS

In Chapter VII we observed several individual writing patterns. Their observable characteristics include (1) variety of topics, (2) definite personality effects, and (3) free exploration of concept and ideas. Also, it is obvious that being able to write in one's own way functions as emotional release.

Several questions pertinent to the teacher's concern for pupil growth may remain, however. For instance, is there any evidence regarding a student's choice of topics, and are topic patterns evident? Another question pertains to increasingly complex (1) use of punctuation, (2) sentence structure, and (3) idea organization. Do they increase naturally? Do they increase as much in a "free writing" situation (where children generally decide what they will write about) as they do when topics are regularly assigned?

A third question concerns the degree to which the writer becomes personally involved in the presentation of her "characters." Does she recognize that human beings, and interaction between human beings, offer increasing possibilities for drama and suspense, or does her main theme remain the *event*?

Still a fourth question remains, and this concerns vocabulary development. It is generally assumed that a person's writing vocabulary is larger than her speaking vocabulary. Does she use meaningful words in her writing that would not commonly be used by a child speaking on her level?

With those questions as a basis for study, the remainder of this chapter will present a selection of twenty stories and poems written by one girl over a period of four years—grades three, four, five, and six. These writings, which represent a cross section of her efforts, are presented in graded order. Many of them are presented with the original spelling. This is an important consideration, because the questions we have asked can best be answered and studied if we are observing original materials. While she was careful later to edit most of the material that was to be used again, only those stories so annotated in this group have been edited.

Grade Three

December

December is a Jolly
Time Christmas is
in the air from
Christmas morning
Till Christmas eve
Christmas is every
were you have
a Tree you
decorate and on Christmas
night you Jast say
good night!

December

December is a Jolly
Time Christmas is
in the air from

Christmas morning
Till Christmas eve
Christmas is every
were you have
a Tree you
decorate and on Christmas
night
you Jast say
good night!

FIGURE 16

Santa Claus

When Santa Claus comes
home at night it is such
a fright he goes to his
small bedroom and say's
good-night!

it was Santa Big reedeer
he was runing away
oh! my reedeer come back
right away!

Christmas eve

There is one very
spcail day in The year
it is Christmas Eve and
it's here!

it's when lets of Things
happand very spcail Things
To! like hanging up
stockings and saying Boo
and when Santa Claus comes that's
Woo!

and every year on Christmas
eve it's so much Fun for
me and I would Think
on Christmas eve all would
have fun around the
Christmas Tree.

The Mystery of Mrs. Square head

Chapter 1

about 7 miles from Birdseye Town, and in a Little square house lived Mrs. Square head her husband was dead and had left a map in The ground so Mrs Square head sayed I am going To make a mystery out of it yes I thing I will make a mystery. So She dug and dug and she got the map and Then she made a mystery out of it, But when She was Sure She can't Read it But when she Started to Read it, it was will here is a picture

Well, what if you had to Read it? But it is in the Sea She said, Well, I will get it, But little did She Know The mr Hotdog was hereing every Thing She Said. He said if I can Just get That map; oh it's 7 I've got to get to bed hoooooooo, When She was a Sleep mr hotdog Tip, Toed in and got The map, and The next morning When MRS Square head wlak up oh it morning So I've got to get on my way So she went To get The map when she saw it was gone oh oh The map oh oh oh oh oh oh I've got to get my Map Back I Think I can remember it, Some oF it

Thats all I can remember I Think oF as She Was Thinking mr hotdog was in hidden Gold Town, By the Time MRS hotdog was asking mr hotdog about The map, mrs Square head was Ther to, as mr hotdog came out Mrs Square head Said get your hands up in The air and when Mr hotdog Ture around MRS Square head had a Gum OK Said mr updog shitering OK gave me The Map OK here it is But That is not The map

YES IT IS
NO IT IS NOT
yes it is
NO it is not

Ok it is not, get me the other one or I will shoot you So he went in get me The map,

here it is.
THANK YOU yes this is the one

Now I Will Be on my way Now all I have to do is get Treasure, now lets see you go wast Then go east Then wast then east and There is The Treasure, She Went for 10 Welks and Then She got on the island She look it over and Said Know one is on This island it dost not have a name I don't Think So I will name it Borden'sbeen I Think I will go around it and as she want around it She sing around the bordenbeen in halfahour around I'll go around I'll go, I like This place noone To say don't do This don't do That so nice and quiet, The all of a sudden she Jumped up and Said,

Mr hotdog
What are you doing here. I am drowning, I not going To hlep you Said mr hotdog and She Said again HLEP hlep hlep hlep BBBBBBBubble. I am Coming, hlep, I am Coming hlep me hlep me hlep me.

Chapter 2

mr. hotdog comes Back.

how did you get here I have a map, I copid it ho I will get you how how how you Just I'll get you so hlep me I will, Than after she said that hlep Now I don't Think That I till you that mrs squarehead was 25 year old so you can Think That every man will you Know What Will mr hotdog fell in Love with her and said will you marry me, Kiss kiss kiss kiss kiss kiss kiss kiss kiss kiss kiss But you are marry I don't love her What you don't love her I Can't I Won't I hate you I hate you I hate you I hate you Smank go a way go go go go go go

Chapter 3

were is mrs saquarehed

The next wlak when By a other man came To island The man came To see Square head, mrs Square head Mrs square head mrs square head may I see you, here I am, may I see you, are you mrs square head, yes I am mrs square head, will your husband lift a will, let me see it, ok, but This saids I am coming To get looo dollars, yes, mr hotdog was hereing every thing She said

[A Story]

Chapter 1

The Talking Books

now once There were 5 books Their name's were "Dictionary" and "The Cat That was clever", and "To The castle" and "Bank Book", and in came "Golden yonDer." Then Ronnie get The "Dictionary," Lynne got "The Cat That was clever," and Carol get "To The Castle and The Banker got The "Bank Book" and Then Jimmy got The "Golden yonDer" Ronnie took alook at the "Dictionary" Lynne took a look at "The The cat That was Clever." and Carol took a looked at "The Castle" and The Banker looked and looked at The "Bank Book" and Jimmy looked and looked at "Golden yonDer," The 5 Books liked To Be looked at. They were happy untill one day every one got out The Books. But They bib not get out The "Dictionary". Everyone was happy. Everyone But The "Dictionary." But Then one day There was one man came in and got out The "Dictionary" so The Dictionary" was happy.

Chapter 2

The new Books

Now one day There was a new Book. But This Book was not like the Other Books. It was a "Magic Book". It had Magic inside it They were All happy it came But All OF The Boys Would want iT. But Then a "Cook Book" came and All The girls picked it up. "Dictionary" and "The Cat That was Clever" and "To The castle" and The "Bank Book" and "Golden yonDer" were very sad Because The Boys and girls DiD not pick Them up. But one day Those Little girls and Boys left The "Magic Book" and "Cook Book" on The Shelf and picked up "Dictionary" and "The Cat That was clever" and "To the Castle" was

Read and All had a Fair turn To Be Read. Then one Day "Dictionary" said "I am going to Be a hero some Day." "How?" said all The Books. "oh I Just am. I want To Be a hero Too." Then one day "To The castle" fell off the shelf "Ohhh! I fell off The shelf." "I am comeing." said The "Dictionary." So Down went the "Dictionary" with his umbrella. "I will Save you." So Down went the "Dictionary." When he landed he landed OK. But The Thing was how To get "To The Castle" up on The shelf. Every one Said "I Don't Know." "Get on The first shelf, and Then The Other and Then The next and The next. "We're here! "I am a hero." "You sure are "Dictionary," Said a Voice. "What is That?" "Oh! It's just one of The Readers." "To The Castle" was very happy, Because "Dictionary" had saved him. "Hurray! Hurray!"

3 Chapter

The Big Fight

The 5 Books were all very happy untit one day There was a Fight. What a Fight! Every one was in it. Bang! Boom! Bang! Boom! Bang! Boom! The "Dictionary" Was very Banged up and So was "The Cat That was Clever" and other 2 Books. But "Golden yonder" did Not have a scratch. "Why don't you have a scratch on you?" "I've been Sitting uphere all The Time." "Gee I wish I was, Too," said "Dictionary" "Look at me." "oh! Said "Golden yonder," "you are a mess, Boy." The other Books were still Fighting. "Oh dear! Said "Golden yonder" and "Dictionary," "Such a pity. They are All Fighting. Lets go Try To Stop Them." "OK!" So down They went. Ba.Ba.-.Bang! "Here we are. But how do we stop them?" "I don't know." "Well we have to stop Them! But how?" So "Dictionary" and "Golden yonder" walked over. "Hey Stop it! Stop it! Stop it!" "STOP IT" Stop every one. Stop! Now Stop This Fighting!" "OK! OK! So up went The Books looking mad at each other. "I'm mad," said "To the Castle" "Oh Be Quiet!" "Ok" don't rush don't rush I am coming I am coming, I don't take that Talk, who is going to stop me, I am said "Bank Book", how Then All of a Sudden smank right square in the kisser ououch OUCH cry to the castle you can't do that to me, Stop me, OK smank miss me he! he! he! All right don't fight we have all ready had one OK lets don't have a other one OK So up They went

4 Chapter

a Thankgiveing Celebration

Then one day There was a lat of noise in the hall. I wonder went is going on. All The Book shrug There shoulders So Golden yonder take a look out the windows. ho ho ho it's Thanksgiveing. no said all The Books let's have a celebration OK What do we do I know I know We can make a turkey OK how do we make it you make a circle A Circle That's like a egg, oh just listened to me, Then you make a head But Turkey Don't have heads on Thankgiveing, But This is not Thankgiveing Oh for get it. OK Lets get to Work OK every one got to work They made a circle and a head although it was not Thankgiveing and They made a Beutiful tile oh That good said Dictionary Thank you said Golden yonder and When To The caslte Saw it he ho most fell oFF The Sherl as he no most fell Bank Book grabbed him, wooooooooooooow you save my life Thank you lets go to wrok OK so oFF They marched over To There places.

5 Chapter

The Big Thing

It was Thanksgiveing Season and all The Books were happy I am happy said all the Books thanksgiveing ThanksGives is here it sure is said Dictionary When Thanksgiveing was over watch was a long Time they were all happy until one day a Smartalex came in it was TV Queen Whataaaaaaaaaaaaaaaau gi gi gi gi gr girl Whats your name, were Did you Come from, how did you get here, Iiiii Justttt gottt hereeeeee Iiiii aaaa newwww Book, after 4 weeks They Love her you would have Ben wll listened I Love you I Love you ho Be still you are always intorrapting me, Ok Go a head Will you will will you marry me, What marry marry you give me time to Think it over, OK, The next day Want By I have deceided I I Will marry you if you will Be good to me, I will Be very good, so They got marry the next day after Dictionary was marry it was 2 years later they had Baby Books oh They were so cute They name Then Booklets Be cause They were twins ho They were so happy living on The sherfs They like Dictionary There Father Daddy Daddy Go here one of The Booklets are Sick Sick Whats going on said TV Queen one of they Booklets a sick SICK get this get that ho my Booklets sick WIII will Will Just sand there.

REACTIONS TO HER THIRD-GRADE WRITINGS

As one reads these writings for materials pertinent to the questions formulated early in this chapter, one has a basis for many reactions. For instance, these writings perfectly typify original manuscript. That is, a child of the third grade would be considered normal if her writings had qualities similar to these.

First, as a child begins to know the differences between the shapes of capital and small letters, she uses both alphabets without much distinction. She eventually learns of the "small *t*" and the "capital T," but she may use them interchangeably at the beginning or in the middle of words *and* sentences. (Follow this development as you read typical writings set from original, unedited manuscript through the next three grades.)

Another characteristic of original writings is misspelled words. Children quite normally attempt to use words in their writings which they have actually had little or no acquaintance with in either reading or writing. Interesting to note are the facts (1) that previous spellings are definitely carried over into attempts to spell other words ("Thank*givei*ng"), and (2) that misspellings recur in like forms until a "more correct" form is learned ("spcail" occurs twice in her first poem as the spelling of "special," a word usually included in sixth-grade spellers).

A third characteristic of development taking place is concerned with punctuation. It is an amazing triumph for a child when she can simply pick up a story she has just written, then interpret the ideas, feelings, and emphases almost flawlessly—without even the most basic punctuation marks! True, a reader other than the writer would be under a considerable handicap, but the important idea here is that the writer clearly knows her intended meaning, even if she has not yet learned the techniques of making it clear to others. Thus the stage is set before we begin much of our "programmed teaching."

At the third-grade level, few lessons have attempted to illustrate punctuation marks and their uses. Writings of most children at this age level are void of commas, question marks, quotation marks, and other types of punctuation—even periods. However, with the apparent need—and with the teacher's help—this growth is ready to take place, and its development should be noticed in the next presentations. (Compare Figures 16 and 17.)

Children read many books, most of them by professional writers. Many of their ideas for the forms of their writings develop from their reading. Typical is the use of "chapters" to give emphasis to *groups of thoughts* and *changes of ideas*. If we recall that, when writing, the child is in the process of organizing her own ideas (and this may sometimes be interpreted as organizing the ideas of others), then we will understand use of chapters or similar sections as part of the growth process.

With those reactions in mind, we now turn to selected writings by the same girl as a fourth-grader.

Grade Four

THE ELECTION

once upon a Time There was a Bear. he was a BBBig Bear. Biger Then all of The oTher Bears, The Big Bear was BRAVE. and one day he met The King of The forest, Leo The Lion. Buster Bear was horified To find the Lion. The lion was thought to Be Braver and Stronger than him in The forest. Then all of a Sudden Buster Bear had and idea he went running away Saying I have it! I have it! I will write a poster it will say ELECTION FOR KING OF THE FOREST

He put the poster on Several trees, then he decided to Campaign all over The forest. he went To houses and Churches and meetings To make Speeches about how Brave and Strong he was, and why he would make a Braver King. then Leo, the Lion decided to Campaign too. Buster pass out cigars to get The animals to vote for him, and Leo Lion Pass out Candy for the baby animals To get there father to vote for him, finally the day of ELECTION OF THE KING, votes kept comin in and Rollo Snake put some in Leo's Box and in Buster too. What a race, They put it in Leo's Box in Buster Box Leo's Leo's Buster Buster. Then he said, "The King is-Wait minute here is anoTher vote, There is NO King. it is a Tie!

NO here is another vote on the floor! The winner is LEO THE LION!

Buster walked Sadly away. wait Said Leo, "I have a good ideal you Be vice-King!" "Oh That is wonderful," squirmed Sammy Worm.

from Than on Leo a Buster were very happy

The End

MISS PEACOCK GOES TO OAK LAKE CITY

Chapter I

In the middle of the park, there stands a little house, just big enough for Miss Peacock, and her bird named Fairy. Now it had been a long time before Miss Peacock had taken a trip. "I have'nt taken a trip for a long time," said Miss Peacock, to Fairy. Miss Peacock took her bird everywhere she went. Thats why they lived happily. Miss Peacock sat down and thought and thought and thought and then she had it! "We'll invite my grandchildren to come and stay with us." Fairy liked the Idea very much, and he showed it by jumping up and down. So Miss Peacock called up and said, do you think it would be possible if I had my grandchildren out." "Oh! I don't mind," said a voice and I am sure my children will enjoy it." "Oh thank you" said Miss Peacock and hung up the telephone. "Fairy! Fairy! they can come," she yelled, as she ran into the kitchen.

"A Long Distance Call"
Chapter II

A day or two later Miss Peacock heard a knock at the door. "It must be my grandchildren. Watch you manners," she said and opened the door. "Grandma!" they yelled, "It is good to see you agian." They ran and said "Hello" to Fairy. "Did you like your trip?" "We loved it." "Oh! that's good," she said, "and no one said any thing for the next few minutes.

Then Miss Peacock and her grandchildren started to talk all together. Then the next day the sun was up and so was Miss Peacock, fixing breakfast, and talking to Fairy. "Don't you think that my grandchildren are nice. "Oh yes," said Fairy. Then at about 11:30 all 10 of her Grandchildren were up. It was before Miss Peacock had known that she had a long distance call. "A man called from Oak Lake City," said the Operater, when she answered the telelphone. "Who is it,"? "Mr. Doghound," "Mr. Doghound! Who is he?" Don't ask me Lady." "Put him on!"

Miss Peacock said "Hello," "Hello Miss Peacock. I'll have to tell you this—your rocks from Jupiter did not come through." "What! It did'nt come through! What could have happened to them?" "It might have been stolen,"

"Oh! No! no! I hope that didnt happen," "I'll be right there," and she hung up the telephone, and said "Carol (that was the oldest grandchild.) I have to go away I want you to take care of your 9 Brothers and Sisters and I can't take Fairy

"Oh! but where are you going",?" I have to go to Oak Lake City", "Oak Lake City!" "That is 100 miles a way." "I know," and she went to get her suitcase and packed and told her,"Don't forget—take care of your Brothers and sisters and Fairy," and slammed the door!

Chapter III

Oak Lake City

Miss Peacock got on the train. "Toot!", "Toooooooot!, toot, toot! tooooooooooooooooooooooot!" The train left the station. On the train Miss Peacock met Mrs Roller. Miss Peacock said "Have some chicken!" She had a lunch Box, with Big Red letters. "Lunch Box" it said. So Mrs Roller Sais "thank you. Thank you very much. I was a little Hungry", "I have got more if you want it". "No thank you." A Half a hour later they came to Oak Lake City. At The Station There was a big piece of paper hanging From a rope. It said, "Oak Lake City." "Well, Mrs. Roller here we are at Oak Lake City!" They all got off and said I liked the ride. Thank you! Thank you very much!"

Miss Peacock got off too and went to the Oak Lake City Hotel. She got Room 8 and She made sure she had a Room by the window. She was tired, so she took a rest and said,"I'll call my grandchildren and see how they are." Then she lay down and went to sleep. A little bit later she was dreaming about a boy who had not had food For 10 days. So she too became Hungry, She went to get Some Food Then she ran, into Mr DogHound, "OH! Mr Houndog, yoohoo, Mr Houndog! I have been looking for you." "Miss Peacock, I have been looking for you Too!" "Oh! we have to Start right away!" So That night they started to look. They looked and looked and looked, "LooK!" Shouted Miss peacock. I found them in this trash can in this alley!" "Oh my rocks from Jupiter," So a day or to later she got on the train and left, When she got home she said "I hope I never have That experience again."

The End

The First Trip to the Moon*

When I was a little boy I always wanted to go to the moon. Well, now I am ten and I'm ready to go. I won First Prize in a contest, and now my plans are made.

My Father drove me over to the Space Station, and I saw the Rocket that I was going to ride in. I said goodbye to Dad and Mother, and to my sister, and the pilot said "Come on. We're ready to leave."

We were ready to leave. "Ten, nine, eight, seven, six, five, four, three, two one. . . .BLAST OFF!!" Well, we were off. I took a glance out the window and I saw a meteor falling. "Look! Look!", I shouted. I was so excited for that was the first time I ever saw a meteor. As we got farther up in space I saw "Leo the Lion" which is a constellation. I was very big and it really looked like a lion. The The Pilot shouted back to use, "Seven thousand miles to the moon!"

"Mr. Walker," I said (you see he was a great scientist who was going along), "Does the moon have any water or life on it?"

"We have never been to the moon, so we don't know if there is, or there isn't," said Mr. Walker. "We don't have very long to wait."

The pilot looked back and said, "Three thousand miles more!" I looked out of the window. "I see it! I see it!"

"Naturally you see it," said Mr. Walker in a disgusted tone of voice. "We can see the moon from earth."

I looked at Mr. Walker puzzled. "Does the moon have robets on it?" "See, it says right here—robots are walking around the

"Let me see that book," said Mr. Walker. " 'A Trip to the Moon!' " He handed the book back to me. "You simple thing! That book isn't right."

"My Dad said it was!"

"Well, your Dad's nuts!"

"That's an insult," I replied and I turned to the window. Just in time, too, because I saw Venus. "Isn't Venus and Mars the planets they think have life?"

"Yes, for the first time your'e right."

———
* Edited by the student.

The pilot said, "Two miles to the moon, now!" ZZZZOOOOMMMM "We're here!"

"Oh, yes, before we go. . . . . I heard on the news that the scientists think it would be easy to live in space," I said.

"Well, there is a possibility of that," Mr. Walker said. "Sam, (He is the pilot) you go out first."

Sam climbed out, then Mr. Walker, then me. "Don't forget your mask," reminded Mr. Walker. "Come on! Come on!"

I jumped out. Boing . . . . boing . . . . boing . . . . boing I jumped around. "What's wrong with this ground?" I wanted to know. "Oh, I remember, it's gravity. The moon doesn't have much gravity." "Do you see any water, Sam?"

He said no, and had to shout it for I couldn't hear too well. "Did everyone forget me?" I said. We jumped around. "Look, Look," I said, "there is some water."

"I see it, too," said Mr. Walker. He jumped over to the spot. "It is real water, and plants are growing around the water." Sam suggested that we see if we could find anymore water and plants. So we all three jumped around some more. Jump, jump, jump, jump! We found some more water. "Look how funny earth looks from up here." "I'd sure like to go to Saturn."

Sam said quickly, "No! My job was to take you to the moon and back safely, and in a hurry. I think we'd better get ready to go back."

I told them to go ahead and leave without me for I wasn't ready yet. At that Sam picked me up and carried me to the Space Ship. I kicked and shouted "Let me go," but that didn't bother Sam.

We took off for earth. An hour or so later I saw the earth Satellite Explorer going around the earth. I looked very funny. It wasn't as round as the Russian Sputnik.

"Three thousand miles to earth," said the Pilot. I thought how I'd been to the moon and on the way back. All of a sudden—"Here we are, on earth!"

I got out, and said "Thank you very much." Then I added, "If you're going to any planets one of these days, let me know. I'd like to go along. Goodbye, and thank you again." Then I saw Mother and Dad and I ran.

"Oh, Mother," I said, "I had the best time. I'm glad to be home, though."

"Well, get in the car and tell us all about it," she said.

The End

A Trip to Saturn*

"Look, Mother," I said. "Look, another contest. This one is advertised by our good friend Chris Roosevelt, and the first prize is a trip to a PLANET!"

"Let me see, dear. All you have to do is write the best reason why you would like to go to Saturn." Mother smiled, "Well now all you have to do is win!"

It took me several days to prepare my essay but at last it was finished. There was still four weeks until the deadline, but I gave it to the Mailman, and asked him to please deliver the letter in person. I told him about the trip to Saturn, and he said he would deliver my contest entry for me.

When the four weeks were up I watched the mail every day. When I had about given up I received a letter addressed to me. And when I tore it open, I was so excited I couldn't talk.

Finally I shouted, "Mother, I won! I won!" Mother was as excited as I was, but then I had to run and tell the neighborhood. I ran out of the house, yelling at my friends, "Ann! Mary! Jim! Patty! David! Come quick. I won! I won! I'm going to Saturn!" They were all happy for me. Ann said, "You will be famous, and sensational."

When the great day came, all of my friends came down to see me leave, as well as Mother and Dad, and my sister. All of the boys and girls shook hands and told me to have a good time, but when it came to Ann, I sort of lost my head and kissed her. My face turned red and I ran to the Space Ship. It was take-off time, and they said "Ten, nine, eight, seven, six, five, four, three, two, one. . .Blast Off!"

---

* Edited by the student.

I looked down at Ann and she looked very little. She waved and then we disappeared.

Mr. Walker and Sam were on this trip, as when we went to the moon. After awhile we passed something familiar—the moon. Sam told us that Saturn was miles and miles, thousands of miles away. I wondered why the Space Ship was going so slow. Mr. Walker told me that when we got beyond gravity the Ship slows down.

We passed the Northern Lights.....They were red, blue, green, and yellow. They were beautiful, and it looked like we were headed right into them. We were blinded and Mr. Walker shouted "Duck"

We passed Mars—it was about two thousand miles away Sam told us. We heard a sudden whistel, and it was a comet falling into space.

Finally, after several hours, ...zoom, zoom, zoom. . . .and the Space ship landed on Saturn. The rings were fabulous. I asked Mr. Walker what they were made of.

"They are particles of dust and other things," said Mr. Walker.

"Well, why is Saturn the only plant that has rings," I said. "My Mother said that all the planets had rings at one time or another."

"Yes, I suppose so," said Mr. Walker.

When we all got out we wanted to go on the rings, and that is exactly what we did. I fell off, but I didn't care because there is no gravity in space, so I floated back up again. Mr. Walker pulled me down where I was supposed to stay or I would have kept right on floating.

We walked about some more, and guess what we saw! A man and a woman. They must have been from Saturn because they sure didn't look like us. Mr. Walker and Sam were both astonished! Sam and I didn't move, but Mr. Walker went right up to them. Sam and I were afraid they might be enemys, but Mr. Walker told us they were friendly. So Sam and I went over to where they were and said "Hi." Sam was scared, and his knees were shaking.

After awhile we were all good friends, and finally Sam was doing the most talking. We talked about planets and how they lived. Sam Said he had a wonderful idea. . . .he was going to ask the people to take us around the planets. When they said they couldn't do this, he said, "O.K., then we'll take you back to earth with us."

The man and woman from Saturn said "No!" We then asked if we could take a picture of them with our camera. We explained what a camera was, and they didn't care.

Sam said it was time to leave, for the Rocket was timed for Blast Off. So I said "What is your names?" The Man said his name was "Screwey" and his wife's name was "Louie." I thought they were funny names but didn't say so. Louie told me that they had gotten their names from a star.

We left Saturn and the beautiful rings, and we were very tired on the way home. Finally we landed on earth, and I said "Thank you and Goodbye." I saw Mother and Dad, but turned around and said to Sam and Mr. Walker, "I don't ever want to go to space again."

But of course, I might change my mind.

The End

WINTER IS HERE*

Winter is here
It is snowing everywhere
In cities, and the country-side
The wind is blowing
But I don't care.
How do I know?
Because I've been playing in the snow.
That's how I know!

WHAT'S UP NORTH!

What's up North
Why Santa Claus
Of Course

---

* Edited by the student.

He has ten
little helpers
and two of
them are hers
With that
Santa Claus
is just a
bundle of
Nerves

Christmas Eve
is here and
Santa Claus is
Ready For
Christmas this
year

IT'S HERE!

It's come your
right its not far
away Thanksgiving.
and Thanksgiving
Holiday

enjoy Thanksgiving
While you can and
The Many blessings in
are land.

and when your
Thanksgiving is done
lets hope that you
have had lets OF
Fun.

A Thanksgiveing Turkey

THANKSGIVING

Thanksgiving! Thanksgiving!
is not far away Thanksgiving
is Fun I always say.

We have turkey and
masked patotos too
Thats what we always
always do

THANKSGIVING

Thanksgiving is gay
I always say in fact
Thanksgiving is right
today

> The Old Boddie
> turkey that once
> was alive is going
> to be right inside

REACTIONS TO HER FOURTH-GRADE WRITINGS

Many noticeable changes have taken place in this girl's writing style during her fourth-grade year. As she has become more able at getting her rather "free-flowing" ideas onto paper, so has she adapted some interesting ways of getting her personal meanings across to the reader.

For instance, at least three techniques for emphasizing words and phrases are discernible. First, she has begun to use capital letters in an effort to "shout" meanings and feeling. In her first story she spoke of the *BBBig* Bear. She also, in announcing the election results between Leo the Lion and Buster Bear, loudly announced that there would be *NO* King—because of the tie in votes. In a third instance, she spoke of a rocket ship that was readying to *BLAST OFF*.

Her second technique for emphasizing her thoughts is perhaps quite related to the first. Occasionally, she would write a word such as HELP over two or three lines, such as—

HELP!

When she read her stories to the class, she certainly gave emphasis to this word!

A third way in which she learned to give emphasis to her meanings was evident. She made increasing use of the exclamation mark during all of her fourth-, fifth-, and sixth-grade years. One can notice how she eventually used the exclamation mark to meet most of her needs for emphasis, while only occasionally using one of the other two techniques at this level.

A writing child—one who is putting her own ideas into written words—is very often an excited child. At times the excitement becomes so great that a word is omitted completely. At other times—and this is especially true with *original manuscript*—the child will begin to spell a word but leave it incomplete to get on to the rest of the idea. This girl, who certainly was capable of spelling most words expected of her, would often spell the word "and" with a single *a*, or "your" with only the first three letters, *you*. Her original manuscript contains many misspellings, as you have noticed. If you need to, compare her original manuscript with her polished stories (those which would be used for contributions to class collections, given away as Christmas presents, etc.). Then too, recognize the great number of words that children from grade one on will try to use in their stories. Some words used by this girl in her original manuscript include *squirmed, horified, election, campaign, operator, have'nt, slammed, experience,* and *dreaming,* only a couple of which are spelled incorrectly.

Let us also summarize some signs of growth in her use of punctuation marks.

1. Capital letters are no longer used in the middle of words.
2. Capital letters are still used occasionally to begin larger and major words.
3. Capital letters now appear at the beginning of almost every sentence.
4. Commas mark nearly all important pauses.
5. Commas occasionally are used to separate "complete ideas" and "related sentences"—probably in spots where a conjunction might eventually be utilized.
6. Quotation marks now appear around what one person is saying.
7. Quotation marks still are plentiful within the paragraph in which several persons' conversations are still included.

These are some of the signs of growth that are indicated by

her original writings in grades three and four. We can be assured that much of this growth was promoted by the teachers who worked with her during those years. Perhaps it is at least as important, however, to notice that the growth patterns in punctuation usage were at this point seemingly secondary to the continuing free flow of ideas.

When a child wants to write, that child is normally interested in improving his writing according to classic structure. The teacher's role is to encourage balance between free expression and structural expectancy.

One other reaction to these fourth-grade writings pertains to the carry-over from other subjects to creative writing. This girl's fourth-grade class had carried out a study on space and rocketry. (She was in the fourth grade during the year in which Sputnik 1 was launched.) Her stories about "A Trip to Saturn" and "The First Trip to the Moon" contain many ideas that had been learned during the unit of study.

Grade Five

BUMBLE, THE BUMBLE BEE, AND SQUISH SQUASH, THAT'S ME*

Chapter I
Bumble has Trouble

Once there was a very small bumble bee whose name was Bumble, and he bumbled all over the place. He was very sad because Spring wasn't here, but one sunny morning Bumble woke up and it was hot. Spring was here, at last! But then, he thought, and realized that the flowers weren't out yet. "Oh, me" said Bumble. "No honey. What will I do for food?" So he flew away. "Look! Look! there is a daisy!" "Bzzzzzzzzzzzzzzz" went Bumble, as he went down to get the honey. "Buzzzz, buzzzzzzzzz." "Yum, yum, YUM!"

The next day when he woke, it had stormed over night. It had been

---

* Edited by the student.

a bad storm, and had washed everything out, including the daisys and other flowers. All except the dandelions. There were dandelions all over the place, but there wasn't any honey. "Oh, dear, what do I do now?" Bumble looked around until he saw me . . . . Squish, Squash, that's me. Bumble saw me running from a blue jay named JJ, and came to my rescue. I was so grateful to Bumble, that I showed him a daisy patch, (Yum, Yum, Slurp) and from that time on we were fast friends.

Chapter II
Friends

So from that time, Squish Squash, that's me, and Bumble were the best of friends. Squish Squash, that's me lived down at the bottom of a tree and Bumble lived in a bee hive up in the top of the tree. We were very happy together. We buzzzzed and squished squashed all over the place. One sunny morning Bumble woke up. "What's up" I said. Bumble replied "The birds are flying around and you'd better stay in your hole so they don't get you. I've been thinking, also, that it will soon be summer and we have to fix an air conditioner in my bee hive and one in your hole." "O.K." I said, and that whole next week Squish Squash, that's me and Bumble sat up the air conditioner in the bee hive and around the hole that I lived in. In a month, or so summer was here, and Bumble was busy buzzzzing around from place to place, while Squish Squash, that's me, squashed around in the dirt.

Chapter III
The Monster

Squish Squash, that's me and Bumble had a good time all summer. Bumble gathered lots of honey and I squished squashed around in the mud and dirt. Fall soon was here, so we took out the air conditioners. Bumble went out for the last time to get some honey to last over the winter, and we ran into Miss Hildegarde, an elderly old lady, who had a long pointed nose. She wore spectacles and had big blue popping eyes. Her teeth were all rotten, and her ears were as big as Dumbo's. Squish Squash, that's me almost fell over in a dead faint when we first saw Miss Hildegarde. "Bumble, Bumble," I said, "what is that? It must be a monster from a horror movie." She saw me squishing along, and said "young worm, what are you doing?" "Well, I-er . . . . Bumble, Bumble come here!" Bumble flew slowly over, and spied a fresh daisy. The only trouble was, it was on somebody's hat. "Yum, yum, slurp, slurp!" "That was good," said Bumble. "What are you trying to do?" said Squish Squash, that's me. "Get us squashed for good?" "No," said Bumble, "I was just hungry."

Miss Hildegarde said, "Welllll! I'm still waiting. What are you doing?" "Well, er, well, er, I was just, I was just . . . . Bumble, you tell her what I was doing," I said, Squish Squash, that's me. Bumble started to tell Miss Hildegarde something but she didn't let him finish.

"Young worm, your time has come. I don't like worms!" She was just about to raise her foot when a strange man came up behind her and said, "Lady, what do you think you are doing? Stepping on a fine American worm?" "Why, no sir, I was just playing with this nice little worm," she said. He said, "Ha! Let me look this up in section three, page nine . . . . people who hate worms! I'm Mr. Doolittle, so come along with me to jail." And away they went. "Shooooooosh!" I said, Squish Squash, that's me. "That was a close one!"

Bumble said, "Are you alright friend?" "I'm alright," I answered, "but I don't want any more close ones like that!" From then on, we were more careful where we went, and Bumble and Squish Squash, that's me lived happy for ever after. And that is a story of a bumble bee and a worm, Squish Squash, that's me.

Hank The Cow and experience with the Fifth grade

You can find Hank sitting in his rocket chair ready to rocketing into space. These were'nt all of Hank's dream's he had many more such as, a great painost, and a star in polo, he loved to take vacation and his best subject in school he got all D's in Spacewonderful isn't it. He started piano when he was 2 and a half, he did'nt like the teacher, she find out that after a felw kicks,

In polo it was a little hard for there was this one elephant named Paul that every time his horse took a step Boom! Boom! Boom went the old Earth, all he could do is holed on For dear Lift, and when it came to vacation it was FIRST CLASS ALL THE WAY.

Hank was terrible smart so he got a job as a Janator a University School, he clean very bodys room until he arived in the Fifth grade it was a mess, that day they had had a party for there teacher mr pease-cow, while he was cleaning he heard anglea cow fighting with tom cow about a dividsion problem it was 2 into 6 anglea cow said 5 and tom cow said 4 they ask Hank and Hank being so smart said 7. "Thanks" said anglea and tom cow. After that Frank cow walk in he was the best polo player in University School Hank noing a little about polo said to Frank "do you want to play a Game," "Sure" said Frank "Stop! you don't have a Elephant named Paul " "No!" "Good I am happy he is'nt on your team cause every time he takes a step the Old Earth goes Boom! Boom! Boom! it is terrible, after they finished the score was 0 to 0. the next day Mr Pease cow walk in and and was reading to Chris cow about space stop I no some about space OK said Chris name the Farest planet away   Jupater right said Chris cow now name the closest planet pluto, as Hank started to walk out Chris cow yelled "STOP" Hank stopped suddenly "What" "Mr. Evens is coming in today stay" OK Hank said. Mr. Evens talk for a hour our Two when he was finish all the cows got up "I did'nt learn much said Ronnie cow did you" she asked Carol cow "No but That Hank Cow did most of the talking" Lynn cow had been absent. and she was going to play For a talent show at school the Fifth grade noing Hank invited him to it she was there that day and played right in the middle of her music Hank jump up "I NO HOW TO PLAY THAT HE YELLED Mr. Janing jump and said I'll SEE YOU AFTER SCHOOL in Mr Janing office he was getting it all right I'll gave you one more Chance, The Fifth grade who were standing outside yelled Huray Huray Mr. Janing upon the door in this case TO THE WORK HOURSE ALL OF YOU "Shee were sorry Hank" they said as the dug the last ditch For today "I am uses to First class all the way oh this is real luxero bed mad of rock thores all over the Floor after there sentence was up Hank left, the fifth grade was sad but he left he had had plenty of Paino space polo and VACATIONING

The End

Herbert The Dragon

Herbert was a terrible dragon who lives on Dragon Island in Dragon South Seas. Herbert had one problem he was just to long, he was just 22 feet. Herbert had trouble's.
He did blow fire from his nose and he did have green skin, but he was just to long.
22 feet went over and over in his mind "how do I become short. So as the days passed Herbert wanted to play with the Other little dragons but all the said were "get out of here we don't want you your to long," poor Herbert. But one find day all the parents of all the little dragons desided to have a prince good idea so the parent conuicl broke up For that day.
Weeks went by but no prince was elected.
2 or 3 weeks passed but no prince was elected, so now it was time for anomanations.
Oscar mother said him and Joe mother said him and finaly someone said Herbert the days passed vote For Herbert came piling in, so Herbert was elected For he was the LONGEST DRAGON on the hole Dragon Island.

The lonely little House

Once in New york City there wasn't big houses but little ones. But as New york grew and grew big buildings were being built. One little green and white house saw all the big buildings going up, "Oh My" said they little house I am going to be a great big building." The next day he thought he was going to be big building but the workers stoped the little house was the only little house in New york City. The big buildings bragged how big a strong they were they little house droped a great big crydrop. day by day the little house begam sadder and sadder. "No one loves me" he said. About a mouth later this old lady came to the big city of New york City her name is Miss lampost, she was looking for a place to stay she did'nt want to stay in a big hotel it was to much money anyway. So She was looking for a place and there THE LITTLE GREEN HOUSE WAS IN FRONT OF HER. She knew that was For her she walk in a everyone was very happy. The old lady had a place to live. The little house someone love him. So they lived happyly every after.

The Mystery of the Missing Spectales

Once upon a time there was a elephant named Elmer, now Elmer noing that he was very near sighted and coud'nt see a thing with out his spectales lost them. He did'nt no where he lost them but he did. So not noing where he lost them he called on stewy the hippo, nobody new the stewy had almost lost all his eye sight. So he said, "can you help me find my spectales." "OK where did you last leave them" Bang "Ouch" stewy said, and a bump arose "what happen Elmer said." Oh I just hit my head on the shower rod" "Shower shower that's where I left then" On The shower Rod" "No silly in the shower, I took a shower this morning "Oh I can't help you there I am to Fat you better call on Ferdinard the horse "Ferdinard can you help me find my spectales I've lost them," "Why sure" said Ferdinard, " "Well" said Elmer stewy, , the hippo you no him don't you? "sure" Ferdinard replyed again "its some where in the shower." About 2 hour later at the bottom of the drain "I can't find them Elmer" Ferdinard yelled up. "What" said Elmer "I can't Find Them" "Ohhhhh" said Elmer well Thanks, let me gave you some advice, "call on the telephone adigal moth because you surely don't want to walk that far." "No" Elmer said. So when Ferdinard left Elmer ran slowly into the house. "Hello is abigal there," "yes speeking." "This is Elmer," "Oh Hello Elmer can I help you", "why yes I have lost my spectales," "why what do you want me to do," "Help me find Them Ferdinard said it be wise, to call call you," Oh well in that case "Sure! but I don't have to go any

where," "why ' where are they," "right up there," and she pointed
towered his head and Elmer falt and they where there "Oh now I
remember I did some paper work and I must a push the up there
Thanks a lat abagal" "yuor welcome" "by" Said Elmer So when he
got home he wrote thank you note to stewy and Ferdinard and so
For a hole week the hole Forest laugh!

On Christmas eve night the Stars shine so bright
with Snow and sometimes mistel toe
then we have to go to Sleep sometimes in bed I Play little bow Peep
then there are 8 tiny raindeer on the roof
then all of a sudden Poof
Santa Claus appeared Santa Claus Santa Claus Santa Claus is here
of Course said Jane I told you he was near
come on we will tiptoe out
then all of a sudden we hear Santa Claus Shout
ho! ho! ho! this is Far little Jim
a boat
So when it Puts it in Water it will float
heres and little doll for bes
So when it gets tryed it can rest
And heres a little ball for bill
So he can Play with it him and little will
well I guess that's all said Old St. Nick
as he gave a jump, up the chimely he went
the time I have spent so away to the sky
Merry christmas to you and good-By.

The End

Merry Christmas to all

My life

I was born in Mount carnmal hospital on feb 8 1948 at 8:00 in the morning or about 8:-0. The last thing I can remember that is really very important is When I was 4 or 5 Archie had Set up a tent and one morning we woke up and went to get some water and a deal Snake was laying by the water trough and I have been afraid of snakes ever since.

I can remember the trips we have taken to the ohio river on a trian when I was 4 and when I was 8-9-10 I can remember the three trips to Washington D.C. and to Canda and florida and the ome other trip I can, remember was when Mom and Dad and Archie when out west I went with my aunt and uncle to west virgina those Mountains and hills I will never forget.

I can remember all my accidents Such as a arrow halfway through my nose and my cut on my foot when the arrow went half way through my mose I learned to stay out of the way of arrows and my foot I cut that on the tractor and I learn to Stay out of the way of tractors that's all that I can remember that is really important

How The Griaffe Got There
Long necks and there Spots

Chapter I
How they got there neck

One bright sunny morning Jerry (he is a giraffe) was laying on some soft grass. Then all of a sudden While he was looking up he saw a big red apple. He got up a reach up has high as he could but that wasn't high enough. So he tryed again. after 15 minutes latter he was getting tryed. So he said "I'll try once more" up he went and he got it. But when he came down the ground being to swing "Oh! dear" Jerry said "the ground is swing back and Fourth."

Jerry stood up "WHAT!" he yelled a ant but it was a grasshopper minutues latter up to Jerry came Elmer Elephant chewing on a stick "a-a-a-a whats Doc'l looking up. "Now, What does that supose to mean" Pull away the clouds I can't see you. Jerry looked down While Elmer looked up. Oh hi they both said together When Elmer saw Jerry with hes neck long he jump.

"WHAT HAPPEN" yelled Elmer loud so Jerry could here him. "WHAT!" yelled Jerry so Elmer could here him "how did you get the long neck" "Well it's a long story A-A-A-A-Shooooo went Jerry "What's wrong you have a cold" "Yes these clouds do it I think where do for a rain," "do you" said Elmer, A day or two latter like Jerry said it rained but it was'nt a normal rain it was a spoted rain.

Chapter II
there Spots

It rained Sugar rain spots Jerry tasted one of the sugar spot he loved then he ate over 500 sugar Spots A day or two latter the 500 Sugar Spots that Jerry ate started two show. There was another rain two days after the Sugar Spot rain There was a very bad rain now it was a terpantine rain it washed all his beauitful Spot away "Oh" said Jerry, It rain turpantine all day his spots had disappered by morning The next week Pasted.

Then it rain caster Oil, but as much as he hated Caster oil he drank it, But one got Stuck, "Oh my darn neck" Jerry Said. Giraffe were supose to have 200 spots but since one got stuck he only had 100,

"I want to be a Giraffe with 200 spots said Jerry So he sat down under a Apple tree. "Oh! me he said, So along came Elmer again "Oh! whats wrong Jerry" said Elmer "Oh its along story" said Jerry, "Well tell me" Elmer said, well it sugar rain and I had all my 200 spots, "Go ahead" said Elmer, "and then it turpantine rianed and it wash them all away and I ate some of these" and he pointed to the caster oil spots. and ate some but one got stuck and now you see why I am sad." "Oh" said Elmer, and besides that I have only got 100 spots now," Oh! Elmer said again in surprise, Then Elmer got a super Idea "PLUNGER!

PLUNGER! he yelled" and ran to get one Plunger! Said Jerry to himself. here said Elmer in a flash open your month, So Jerry open his month. PLUNG! PLUNG! and he swollowed it 101 spots a pack up the rest of them, "I did it I did it he yelled 200 SPOTS" So he lived happly ever after

The End

The life of a peanut

Penelope Peanut was sitting on her door step when Perry Peanut came running up, "Penelop run the Peanut vender is coming and he isnt seiling Peanuts." "Oh" said Penelope and she jump up. "that shound be fun." "go right ahead I am staying right here."

As soon as the Peanut vender arived at the door step, Penelop jump up "Oh Mr Peanut vender stop I want to go along" "Oh that's nice he said in a sly voice come with us."

So he pick her up a through her in, "Oh Paul she said how nice to see you here" "Oh nice to see you here to he said in a low voice and a disgusted on to."

Lynne look over and started to run away when Penelope got sight "Stop" she yelled. Lynne stop with one Foot up in the air, "Yes" she said "How are you" "Oh find until today I feel a little stick" "Oh that to bad" "John Ronnie Where is Debbie " Debbie peds teddy on the arm, "get off she yelled, teddy jump up "what happen," you are sitting on me you shound be Bang! Becky Fell over Chris "Ouch" she said "Why did you do that" then Debbie said more careful finishing the sentence she started beFore Becky Fell over Chris then Susie and Kay came riding home on Franks trunck—singing For hes a jolly good Fellow with a bottle of Old Cow. Then the next freighting thing was John tewell was preposeing and Ronnie said "Oh yes John Yes John Yes John No! Clap and Ronnie got up aleft.

A week latter they arived a the Factory the Fight they all said "I want a tour First" "OK" he said in a sly voice again." When they were going along they ran into a Detour sign the always
Obey for one time the did'nt and ran into a
tire Factory and the almost was the in.

But they should have done it this time the walk right into the chrushing machine Pam was the First one a just when the thing was two inchs way Bang Paul was broke into little peices "well don't stand there" said one half of his head "get me out of this mast" John run a get some glue Penelop said "here put the ear here and nose here and the mouth and eyes here by the time they where done Paul had eyes were where the mouth was sapose to be.

A year latter they had not been crush yet! Well by the time they where off the Detour they were in the crushing Maching I hate to say this but the next place they where was in Peanut better. AND THE NEXT PLACE WAS in Mr PEASE *MOUTH*

The End

REACTIONS TO HER FIFTH-GRADE WRITINGS

As she continues to write, she quite naturally continues to develop personalized techniques that give emphasis and definite meaning to her style of expression. She continues to create emphasis in a single word (Welllllll!); her use of the exclamation mark is both more accurate and more frequent; her way of using points in sequence (. . . .) along with an occasional dash to indicate pauses and breaks is extremely helpful in creating "expression." One specific incident that comes to mind is characteristic of her growth in these developments.

One day she approached her teacher while in the middle of a story, and said: "Mr. Pease, how can I do this? I don't want to completely come to a stop by using a period. I just want to kinda pause, or hesitate." At this point her problem was presented to the class, and before many minutes had passed the discussion of various techniques that she and others could use in such instances had taken place. The uses of commas, colons, semicolons, dashes, and points in sequence were considered as possible solutions to her problem.

This incident is typical of the way in which children explore writing. They meet many situations which are new to them, and in their explorations they get involved in many situations which become, for the teacher, "teachable moments."

Another noticeable development concerns the girl's ever-increasing accuracy in the use of capital letters. Some of her emphasis techniques still employ capital letters, but most of the capital initials that she uses are used correctly, according to structural expectancy.

In her story "Bumble, the Bumble Bee, and Squish Squash, That's Me," a typical and wholesome reaction took place. Usually these stories (at least of this length) take several days to complete. A child will write a page or so each day, and if a sharing time is provided (to promote both motivation and reinforcement of writing habits), the story will be shared with classmates *as it is being written.* In this instance the phrase "Squish Squash, that's me" was highly approved of by her mates—and usually brought hearty chuckles from them whenever she read it. The development of the story quite naturally included increased use of that phrase, as the reader can see.

The story about Hank the Cow is included to illustrate another popular "success" technique. After several class members and administrators became involved in her story, her classmates showed increased interest in such ideas as (1) what would happen to them next and (2) *how* others would be included. Several others had written stories of this type before she tried "Hank the Cow," and several others tried the same type afterwards. An important development is her attempt to express her impressions of actual persons and events around her. Prior to these fifth-grade stories, many of her writings were based on imagination and fantasy. In this one she is making a change toward a much more realistic theme in her writing; this theme is well illustrated by the following sixth-grade stories.

Grade Six

Deadly Island*

As the clouds parted and the fog lifted, the moon shone down on a small island in the middle of the Pacific Ocean. The waves pounded in and made a thundering sound that echoed through what used to be a deserted island, but now three strangers lay in exhaustion on the water-beaten shore.

Within the next three hours the ocean started it's release of the sun and it made it's horizon. The horizon was filled with artistic colors that seem to blend with the ocean.

With the coming of morning the three strangers who had been ship-wrecked slowly awoke. Marie started to shake Tim and Jerry to notify them that morning had come, and to discuss their problem of what they should do, when she saw something that alarmed her. A giant turtle was approaching.

When the turtle was upon her his neck projected out, and with a cry of pain she fell to the sand. Tim and Jerry awoke with a start, and saw the giant turtle approaching, but had no defense. What were they to do?

Jerry saw some of the wood that floated in from the shipwreck about three feet away. He had to make a quick decision. He decided to grab the wood, so he waited for his chance. He leaped, praying that it would work, because they would all be dead, if it didn't.

He reached the wood, but the turtle seemed to sense his action and hurried forward. Jerry lifted his hand and suddenly the turtle was lying on what now was blood stained sand. Marie got up and saw the turtle, and she turned her head and started crying in relief. Tim and Jerry comforted her.

Soon their curiosity overcame them and they started to explore the island. They had walked only about one-half mile when Tim yelled. Jerry turned around and saw Tim lying down in a snake pit.

It was all a nightmare to Marie. She knew that the sea had once

---

* Edited by the student.

more captured another ship but it failed to capture the three strangers who were now in a frantic puzzlement about what to do.

The snakes were closing in. Tim had just discovered that his ankle was twisted from the fall and it was very painful. They had to think fast because the snakes were approaching faster, but then Marie suddenly saw something and she yelled, "Look!" A vine was swinging in the breeze. She ran and soon it was clutched in her hand.

Meanwhile, Tim was halfway up out of the pit when he started to slip. Then he saw the vine swinging in front of him. The snakes seemed to be coming faster and Jerry and Marie gave a mighty pull and Tim was lifted out just in time. When he reached the top his forehead was wet with perseperation.

They decided to go on, not knowing what awaited them. Within the next three hours the ocean started to swallow the sun and a black velvet cloth started to cover the enormous sky once more.

The three strangers lay on their backs watching the stars twinkle out, one by one, and talking about how to get off the doomed island where they had been thrown only 24 hours before.

The next day the ocean failed to release the sun and fog covered the doomed island. Jerry said, in a suggestive tone, "We need to find a place for shelter."

So they set out to explore the island once more. They found a small cave on the north side, not too far from where they had landed when they were shipwrecked. It was in a mass of bolders. They explored the cave and then the bolders, not finding much. They made a small, but cozy, cave cabin. That night they had made a warm, flickering, fire, and Marie started to tell a story.

"Once my grandfather told me about when he was sailing his ship, "The Knowledge." Grandfather said that he had sighted something off the starboard bow. He didn't know just what it was, so he called to his first Mate, asking him to spotlight the object. But before the light could reach it, the object was gone. Fifty three years later another ship on the same course spotted the same object, but he did more than just spotlight it, he marked it on his map as an island. So what could have happened in those fifty-three years? Scientists think that it must have been a SINKING ISLAND, which had disappeared after Grandfather had seen it, then had risen again fifty-three years later."

Marie finished her story and wished she had a cool, refreshing drink of water to trickle down her throat, but they were surrounded by salt water.

The boys decided to take a watch, to make sure nothing would happen while the other two slept. Tim was first watch. He found it hard to stay awake for the island breeze seemed to soothe him to sleep. The fog parted and the stars and moon shone brightly, just as they did the night they arrived.

The next morning it was clearing so Jerry and Tim went fishing to see if they could get anything to let their stomachs expand. To go with their fish, Marie found some huge, white, bird eggs, so she called to Jerry and Tim and soon the three were collecting the eggs.

All of a sudden a larg black spot appeared in the sky, but they didn't realize what was happening until they heard the loud flapping. Tim yelled "Duck," and they all did, just in time! The eggs had belonged to a large flock of birds that almost killed them. And as good as those eggs might have tasted, they knew their lives meant more. They returned to the cave.

That night it was Jerry's watch, and he was just about to fall asleep when he heard a roaring sound. Was it rescue, or was he imagining things? The sound grew louder and louder. Tim and Marie woke from the noise.

The three of them ran out of the cave, and when they looked up they saw the flickering lights of an airplane. They yelled until they were hoarse, but of course it didn't do them any good. The engines were too loud and their voices couldn't be heard, so the plane passed over them, not aware that the three strangers were still alive. So back into the cave they trudged once again, and their thoughts were not hard to imagine.

The next morning the ocean had once more done it's job in releasing the sun. Marie was the first to awake and she stepped outside to get some fresh sea air, when all of a sudden her scream of fright aroused the boys. They came running to her side, and shared her amazement that half of their island was lying under the salty ocean.

"Where is it? Where is it?" she cried. She ran to the edge of what was left of their island. Time voiced a discouraging thought, "What if this is the island that your grandfather saw, Marie?" Jerry and Marie looked at each other and their faces grew pale. As they returned to the cave the worried look was still there.

In the meantime, back in California the news had already spread and the U. S. Coast Guard was searching for them. One day a man fishing from a small row boat had found a piece of driftwood in a small bay and took it to the Coast Guard office. They checked the direction from which it came, and then re-routed their ships south to search for missing persons or those who might have survived the shipwreck. The message went out over short wave radio.

The three strangers were in frantic need of water. When they were out walking Jerry's eyes lit up like colored marbles. He had sighted a refreshing waterfall, and they all were reminded of crystal clear drinking water that would trickle down their throats. The water was deep, cool, and blue, and Tim wouldn't wait and took a long drink. "Salt!" he shouted and they felt doomed.

That night Thor was angry and showed his anger through a stormy night. The next morning the hot sun had dried out the wet island, which had submerged another twelve inches. When Tim awoke he became hysterical. Jerry and Marie tried to comfort him, but he paniced. He walked close to the slippery, mossy, edge of the island and suddenly slipped. Marie was startled to see a shark rushing to the spot where Tim fell into the water, and before Jerry or she could reach him, flesh and blood were floating on the water. They were too late.

Jerry and Marie were stunned. Now what were they to do. They had no hope of rescue and needed water desperately.

That night when they were lying on the floor of their cave they heard vibrations. Jerry roused up and walked out into the stary night, and there—coming toward them was a U. S. Coast Guard cutter. Here was rescue! The only difficulty being that the board couldn't reach them because of the rocky shoreline. They left and indicated that they would send for help. Jerry and Marie returned to the cave.

The next morning the white clouds were moving across the deep blue sky. They found a package of food that the ship had thrown them, and most welcome was the vacuum of cool water. They drank their fill then ate sandwiches, and candy bars. This was to last them until rescue.

The next morning they were up early, but by noon nothing had happened. They began to get worried, but in the distance they heard a loud roaring sound.

They were excited and within five minutes they could see the U. S. Army Helicopter hovering above them. The helicopter lowered a ladder and a man came down to help them. Marie went up the ladder first, and the man came back for Jerry. Jerry was insistant that the man go back ahead of him for he was a big boy and didn't need help.

Jerry had almost reached the top of the ladder, and had just reached for the door, when his hand slipped. A scream of terror came from Marie when she saw his body lying on the bloos stained rocks that had once kept them alive. Now, there was no need to make an attempted rescue, for the island was now disappearing from view. It had really been the SINKING ISLAND, and Marie was rescued just in time.

The Army helicopter returned with Marie the only survivor of the three strangers. She, alone, had conquered the Deadly Island.

The End

I saw the teeth of death

It was a spring day as two men looked toward the challaging Mountain infront of them. They were both eager to reach the top they started up the rugged Mountain Each man comtinuety kept reaching for the next rock. The day grew warmer as the heads became wet with swept, but they were determined to reach the top They reach the first plato. It was a largh platform with largh jagged rocks. But it was'nt until the second plato that Jack the youngest Slip! it was lucky that the first platform was there and the Jack was a parachuteshoot jumper, he only suffered a painful broken leg. He cound hardly go ahead for his whole body was parolized. Jack yelled up in a faint voice "get help" Sam refused at first for he would'nt leave his partner. But Jack insisted so Sam did so Now Jacks emotion were usually handled in any small cases. It was about two hours after Sam had left, when Jacks hands began to tremble for no reason at tall, he began to jump at any little thing that happen.

All of a sudden his emotions burst out in a terriozeing yell "He won't come back Help! Help! He crawed to the edge of the rock platform, he look over into the vast expands of land below his voice echoed back still with the terriozing sound within it a cold chill ran through his boby. Suddenly Jack saw a site that was hard to believe. A largh mountain lion was approaching.

It's green eyes sparked with the suns rays. Suddenly a feeling of cold fear ran through Jack as the Mountain lion took six largh steps nearer to his parolized body. Jack turned around and saw the four sides of the platform on three sides was a cliff which to Jack right now look bottemless below on the farth side jagged rocks and a hungry mountain lion. Jack looked down thinking it would be better to jump then be eaten when he looked down he saw four small figers at the moment he could'nt tell if the were human or not.

Jack gave a long yell for help! which echoed. It was the echo that Sam heard, so Sam immediately started up the Mountain in search of his partner The mountain lion having sensitive hearing back away from the loud echo. Jacks emotion were in a state of relief now for he new help was on it's way. But Suddenly he remember the Mountain lion. Jack not remembering how far it had been up the Mountain threw a stine the mountain lions mouth open with angry he hesitated Jack began to laugh and sayed "you can't eat me helps comeing Sam well save me."

The mountain lion was full of anxiety to get his largh sharp teeth in the soft flesh of Jacks body Jack Suddenly realized what he had done and that Sam would'nt be there until at least a hafe hour. The mountain lion approached. Jack yet out a desperate Cry for help! his cry reverbarated from the opposite Mountain The mountain lion back away Jack notice this and took advenage of it and gave out another loud yell. Jack continuely repeated the cry until he saw Sam last the ten to eleven feet away the Mountain lion realized he was trap and headed towards the cliff and Jack.

Sam not having any defence jump down to the platform in rescue of Jack. Jacks eyes were blood shot red and his body turning pail Same had now jump upon the lion and they both were fighting for there lives they rolled near the edge of the cliff and were at the very edge when San pulled the largh mountain lion back again the rolled near the gagged rocks Sam Shirt was rip and was stain with blood the mountain lion continuely pierced his claws into Sams body. Sams crys of pain brought Jack to a dission he took his hands and reached for a largh Sharp pointed rock! Jack was fortunate for it came off easely The Mountain lion was upon Same now Jack took close ame at the lions forehead and in a Split-second the lion was lying on the rocky ground which was now almost covered with the lions blood!

Jack gave a laugh he said to Sam there going to have to carry us both back on strapshers! Within in the next 24 hours Jack and Sam were both lying in centeral hospital. Sam was almost a sleep when he gave some reasurring words to Jack we did'nt conquer it this time but there also a next time both Same and Jack eyes closed slowly as they dream of challinging the Mountain once more.

The End

Elmo the Hippo

It was in darkest Africa. When the earth trembled with a thundering sound. I grab the nearest rubber tree but the only Unfortunately thing was that it did'nt have any solid roots. So I ended up bouncing down a small hill into the Nile river.

When I arived up at the top of the water I saw a site hard to believe. A hippo in bright red firey shorts and he had a shiney Sliver whistle tied around his neck, he was sitting in a solid rubber tree! He could'nt be but he was a LIFEGUARD but he was a hippopotamus.

I swam to the nearest hippo and asked if guess was right, I was, he went by the name of Elmo the hippo. I swam up to the sandy beach and asked the so called Elmo what he was doing he replied to me "I am the lifeguard here I guard the hippo's to see that none of them drowned do you what are race to be wash out!" I did'nt answer because I still was in a dizzy puzzlement. What is a hippo doing as a lifeguard, I wondered to myself.

All of a sudden streak of lighting strok across the sky, the water filled Clouds Clashed togather and buckets of rain started to pour down. Elmo blow his shiny silver whistle an each hippopotamus lined up, he began to count 1, 2, 3, 4, 5, 6, this went on until he reached the last few numbers 95, 99, 100 where's the 1 hundredth one, where is blubberball. He was'nt there.

The thought ran through Elmo's mild and I do mean ran because before Elmo could think of a Idea he was out searching for little blubberball. He search as far as he could but the Nile riber is lang and Elmo grew tired rapily. But night was approaching and Elmo discided to reture to the camp because he could'nt see him at night even if he tried.

That night was lang for Elmo he dreamed of blubberball he was probably dead or bleeding to death. Elmo was miserable. Suddenly he had a discoraging thought "what if they take away my shiny whistle and my red firey shorts. Elmo woke with a startle, it was just 3:00 A.M. but he could'nt sleep any longer. He head down toward the nile river and ther he wash he face. Although the nile was muddy he could see his reflection in the Moonlite water.

The next morning the beauiful horizon came up over the african rubber trees. Today, Elmo was determined to find Blubberball. While he was gone Blubberball's sister appeared in the sence with her new boyfriend. They both wanted to no where Blubberball was so I told them I said "his in the nile hunting for him" "hunting" she said as she bursted in to tears. "Is he lost" she said sobbing. "I am afraid so" I said. Bubbleburst her boyfriend did'nt seem to excited about I guess he just didnt like me. "When do you think they'll be back?" "I don't no far sure."

Butterball went into a panic she ran and took along leap for the water. She reach it for the whole 99 hippo's left felt the water. Butterball landing in a belly-smacker. It was to late to help her for the whirlpool had all ready taken her down.

Meanwhile Elmo was still searching, he was as far up a Egypt and still no luck. It was noon now and Elmo stomach could be heard for miles. A native along the banks thought it was a tribe ready for war.

All of a sudden Elmo heard this enormos bello. Was it Bubberball? or was he just imagining things.

Elmo listen closly but could'nt hear any thing but himself treading water. Suddenly he saw Bubberball playing like Tarzan all of a sudden he slip and there was a sudden crash. Elmo grab him by the pants and kick him all the way back to camp. It was disk now and ever body was exhausted I discided to head back for the United States and let Elmo watch his hippo's.

Foolish Fisherman

A largh fish net was thrown out at sea. Every sailor was hoping that they would have a largh catch, for last time theyed only caught about two-hundred-fifty and that would'nt be enough to supply the waiting families.

It was a beauiful day. The sky was clear except for the enormos sun that filled the area with warmth. The Spot the captian had picked was'nt to succussful, for they had been there five hours and only had had a few bites. So the captain inspected the map and discided to go some were around Peru.

They arived, and once more set out their nets. A man standing on a largh box, was tossing out small bits of food that the tuna would enjoy. Suddenly they all had a strike the tuna were biting like mad. Tons and tons of tuna were falling off the fishermans hooks into a largh pool that preserve them until they arived back in home port. The strike continuted until three o'clock that after noon by now there were to many tons to imagine. The captain gave a signal to pull all lines up and head for home, which ever ome did except for one who was determined to catch another. As the motor roared the one fisherman still held his line ferm.

The ship began to move but soon stop. The mem heard a clogging sound. The foolish fisherman tryed to pull his line up quickly before the others found out what he had done, but it was caught fast in the motor. He drop his pole in the water and hurried with the others. The captain gave a order to his first mate to put on his diving suit and see if he could fix the troble. The moon was becoming clearer now night was soon to fall.

Suddenly you could hear the splish of water as the first mate submarghed. The water was a deep blue. The first mate saw the troble right away and tryed to fix it. It took at least a half hour. Soon the exhaused first mate climbed aboard the boat.

It was now night, for the stars and moon shone on the homeward bound fishing boat. On the way the captain did a little investacating. the one fisherman stood in a small conar trembling, for if the captain found out he would dismissed from this job and any other fishing job he might get.

The captain arived were he was standing. The captain was a wise old man and could see the fear in his eyes. The captain asked in a soft toned voice "did you do it." The salior answered in a timed voice "yes". "you no what this means don't you". "yes" he answered faintly.

The ride was short for the frighten fisherman for it seemed they were in homeport in no time. Soon he was walking off the gangblank on to the rickty boarded dock. This was the only job or life carl new.

The next morning he rented a small row boat, he headed out towards the canel. It was noon when Carl got a enormos bite. The fish gave a mighty battle. Suddenly it gave a largh jump, it was at least four feet long. His eyes lite up when he saw the size of the largest fish he had ever saw in his life. The thought ran through Carl's mild that he would show the others, so he tryed his hardest. Some of the largh fish's blood had spread over the area and drawn two sharks about three feet dwon they were circleling waiting for the fish to drop the young inexcperience fisherman was determined to catch the fish weather it meant life or death. Thats what he thought, but when soon he was less the a foot away a coming easly.

Now the fish was near enough so he could tell its dementions. The fish gave a might pull and both Carl and his boat plughed into the ocean. As he went under he saw the terrorizing site of two man eating sharks, that were ready to have a meal. Carl headed for the top. When he reach the top he saw the fishing boat. He yelled tell his lungs were num. The Sharks were least then a foot away from his legs. The boat dip their nets, but it was'nt soon enough for the Sharks had already over come him, and his blood was being tossed around in the red stired up water the fisherman were to late.

The fisherman were all sitting on the edge of the boat. Silence

spread over the it. They had just faced a horrible experience of death.
and fisherman who had like Carl a lot began to recite: "I, A FISHER-
MAN AWAKE TO THE EXCITMENT OF THE SEA, EVEN OVER LOOK-
ING THE TERROR AND FEAR THAT COME BY IT: SUCH IS MY DESIRED
FATE: NO WORLD MORE THAN THE SEA FASCINATES ME WITH IT'S
BEAUTY AND MYSTERY LET IT BE MY GRAVE*

THE END

---

* The student wrote and edited this epitaph before presenting it
to the teacher.

Figure 17

REACTIONS TO HER SIXTH-GRADE WRITINGS

Many tendencies are evident as we view this child's written efforts over a period of four years. Improvement, often in tremendous proportions, has appeared in all the mechanics of expression. Perhaps even more important for the twelve-year-old, however, is the improvement that has occurred in her style of expression.

Her ideas are well formed and, within a paragraph or story, are very cohesive. Her plots have become progressively more complex and realistic—to a level of insight concerning human beings and events that enables her as she writes to explore her own environment easily.

In her original copy of "I saw the teeth of death," she gave one of her best demonstrations of interesting word usage. Her words and phrases included *parolized body, approaching, reverbarated, continuely* (for *continually*), *anxiety, reassuring words,* and *challenging mountain.* Only two of these words are listed in their exact form (*continually, anxiety*) in the new *Iowa Spelling Scale,* which lists 5,507 of the most commonly used words in written materials. Yet she used them, and usually with the correct spellings.

That she is sensitive to her ideas, extremely so, is illustrated by an incident.

She had been writing on her story "Foolish Fisherman" for three or four days when she came to her teacher. She wanted an idea for "an ending." She knew Carl would drown, but that kind of ending would not be appropriate, she thought. It was suggested that she might write something that would serve as "an epitaph for a fisherman." Next afternoon her teacher, as he helped one of her classmates with some ideas, was stooping over the classmate's desk. All of a sudden the girl working on the "Foolish Fisherman" arose from her chair, exploded across the room, and with her right arm released several pounds of tension on the seat of teacher's trousers. After doing so, she stood aghast, with open mouth and hands raised to face, waiting for what was surely to come. Actually, she proved not to be nearly as excited as her teacher was when he accompanied her to her desk to check the ending of "Foolish Fisherman"; such sensitivity is not commonplace.

A SUMMARY STATEMENT

SEVERAL ideas and issues pertinent to the development of creative writing patterns have been presented in the preceding chapters. That these ideas can meet with further testing is reason enough for their presentation. That these ideas can serve as stimulus to other programs attempting to develop creative writing patterns is a second, and very valid, purpose for their presentation.

One question remains. As the teacher attempts to help each child develop fully, what should her efforts be? In other words, how can the teacher best help each child to achieve his potentials as a growing person?

At least four characteristics of creative development appear readily, each of which must become related to the teacher's role.

First, the teacher must help the child to become more autonomous in his own environment. The child must become a decision maker—and he must become a critic of past decisions, so that future decisions will be those that will benefit himself, his society, and both self and society. That the child will make decisions in his creative writing efforts is evident. He will choose topics, ideas, related readings, and other phases of both writing and sharing.

Second, the teacher must help the child to become tolerant of ambiguities both in himself and in others. If the standards of other children differ from the standards of the writer, a positive move of either tolerance or adjustment will allow further progress. If a cleavage exists between the writer's standards and his abilities, too severe self-criticism will more endanger growth than enhance it.

Third, the teacher must help the child to gain personal insights to himself, especially as to how he can better relate to his environment. How can a student best contribute—as a writer or in some other way? Can writing become a method of releasing tensions? Can writing be a way of actually learning about the environment? Does this kind of exhaustive exploration of a person's experience help in self-understanding? That these questions have positive answers is known. The teacher can help students discover similar answers for themselves.

Fourth, the teacher must help the child to become increasingly aware of his experience. That is, the child who more keenly perceives his environment will be more likely to develop fully within it. The child who is most open to his experience will be able to view his experience more objectively and, thus, with more stability. By encouraging free exploration of ideas in a writing program, the teacher is also encouraging the child to make use of his personal awarenesses and perceptions.

In summary, the teacher's role in developing creativity is characterized by helping children to fully utilize *what they already are*. By helping rather than by telling or letting, the teacher will best provide the environment wherein the individual can grow and prosper.

INDEX TO MAJOR CONCEPTS